"ON a walking trip you know that after the right foot it's the left, and vice versa. Beyond that anything can happen."

—*Elisabeth Larsh Young*

HE wonderful gypsy spirit that led a Cedar Rapids, Iowa, family to trek hundreds of miles through several French-speaking countries is captured in FAMILY AFOOT. Jim and Elisabeth Young took their first family walking tour when their children Dave and Eve were aged ten and six. It was a matter of honor for them not to travel by wheels—no mean feat with two children in tow!

FAMILY AFOOT describes the four summer walking trips when the Youngs averaged 75 miles weekly. Their travels took them through the Gaspé, Canada, area (103 miles), across France from the English Channel to the German border (470 miles), through French Canada from Newport, Vermont, to Quebec and Montreal (425 miles), and through the French Pyrenees from the Atlantic to the Mediterranean (504 miles). They hiked across every sort of terrain in weather ranging from drought to downpour. Their unofficial motto was "To let the unexpected happen to us."

Walking across France from Normandy to the German border requires good organization as well as stamina. Elisabeth Larsh Young describes how the family managed to travel so light, stay so healthy, and protect their valuable feet on long-distance walking tours. Her accounts of the sometimes bizarre people and situations the Youngs encountered make this an enjoyable book for all ages—activists and armchair adventurers alike!

FAMILY
AFOOT

ELISABETH LARSH YOUNG

Iowa State University Press, Ames

ELISABETH YOUNG was born and raised in San Francisco and was graduated from Stanford University. In 1948 she and her late husband James moved their family to Cedar Rapids, Iowa, where she now lives. Grandmother of two, she regularly walks twenty-five or thirty miles a week, swims five or six, and finds time to participate in musical, church, and other community activities. *Family Afoot* is the first writing she has done since the late fifties. Her novelette, *Counterclockwise*, appeared in Martha Foley's *Best American Short Stories 1960*.

Maps by Linda Emmerson
Illustrations by Annice Frederick

© 1978 Elisabeth Larsh Young
All rights reserved

Composed and printed by
The Iowa State University Press
Ames, Iowa 50010

First edition, 1978

Library of Congress Cataloging in Publication Data
Young, Elisabeth Larsh, 1910–
    Family afoot.

    1. Voyages and travels.   2. Young, Elisabeth Larsh,
1910–   I. Title.
G470.Y63   910'.4 [B]   77–12225
ISBN: 0–8138–0615–1

To Jim

CONTENTS

INTRODUCTION / Trivet Magic   viii

Part I   AN INEFFECTUAL LADDER
           Mama's Pet Idea   3
           Bad Luck and More Bad Luck   7
           Bitten but Not Beaten   10

Part II   BIGGER AND BETTER
           Normandy Landing   15
           A Prize Squash   20
           Mama Acquires a Major Key   24
           Champagne Find   27
           In Fulsome Praise of Waterways   31
           Birthday with a Twist   35
           A Good Question   38
           Troussey, Unique Troussey   41
           Daddy Gleans a Nugget   43
           Finish with a Flourish   48

Part III   NEW ENGLAND TO NEW FRANCE
           Off on a Zigzag   55
           Another World, Another Time   56
           An After-Dinner Din   62
           Felled by Fries   68
           Sign of Inattention   71
           After Wolfe, Youngs at the Door   75
           An Old Love Affair   79
           Upstream and Upset   81
           Pulp and Pomp   84
           Four on a Vow   87
           The Crunch   90
           Hat Overboard   93

Part IV   SOUTHERN CROSSING
           Knave and Hero in One   97
           Satan, Santiago, and Shakespeare   102
           Juerga by Chance   106
           The Man Who Couldn't Stop Talking   109
           A Great Oak   113
           Independence Day and a Reckoning   116
           Race Problem   120
           Prime Climb   122
           A Dangerous Bull   127
           Béarn Behind, Bigorre Before   129
           Bowl and Pitcher Paradise   133
           Gain a Shawl, Lose a Napkin   136
           Mama's Stomach Does Flip-flops   139
           A Cavey Birthday   142
           Divide Conquered   144
           Après le Déluge   147
           To Eat Is to Make History   149
           To All Good Things . . .   151

ON a summer afternoon, my husband and I, knapsacks on our backs, were walking a narrow, remote road in south central France. To our right a mountain stream tumbled over its rocky bed with a muffled rush of sound; at our left rose a series of cliffs, gray pink in the late sun.

We walked in silence, each with his own thoughts.

We rounded a bend, and, instead of the bare cliff at our side, there was a dense wall of vegetation: underbrush, saplings, and vines. Above it, the cliff.

We had almost passed this thicket when a dog's petulant bark cracked from behind it.

"What's a dog doing in there?" I said.

"Let's find out."

Pushing and squeezing our way through the brush, we found ourselves in a snug gypsy encampment. Besides the black mongrel lying under a dilapidated wagon, there were a man and a woman. We hadn't quite finished taking in that much when, at arm's length from us, an enormous black crow took off from his perch with great commotion and much flapping of wings. Startling to say the least.

The woman—could she have been anything but a gypsy?—was wearing a bright green skirt and an orange blouse. In a dirty, unhealthy way she was handsome. Her silver brooch, bracelets, and long ropy necklace caught my eye. They were simple, rather heavy, the kind of thing I might have chosen for myself. Her hair, which was nearly black, with strands of white, hung across her shoulders in two heavy braids.

Above all, as she came toward us, she had a fine, proud gait.

We exchanged greetings. Her French was excellent.

She told a long and complicated tale of a car breakdown. They needed, she said, forty thousand francs to have their car repaired. (We saw no car—only three or four shoddy two-wheeled open wagons.)

INTRODUCTION / *Trivet Magic*

Car repairs are high, but for forty thousand new francs, they could have bought two or three new cars. Like so many people we encountered in rural France, she must have been reckoning in *vieux* francs, worth a hundredth of the new ones.

Jim asked if there were others in their group.

"Nous avons six enfants." They had six children.

The man had been listening from where he stood beside the smoking coals of a small fire. About this time he approached us. The children, she was saying, were out searching for things to sell. (*"Stealing* things to sell," cynical Jim cracked later.)

"We need to buy a donkey," said the man. Evidently he hadn't heard her say they needed money for car repairs. He was a brigand-ish-looking fellow with less dignity than his wife, unshaven and with bloodshot eyes. His shirt and pants were ragged and patched.

Jim offered them some of his Gitane (Gypsy) brand cigarettes. ("Never thought I'd be giving Gitanes to *gitanes*." he said later.) The man lit his. The woman stowed hers somewhere in her blouse.

My husband had a suspicious streak in him. Beginning to doubt they were real gypsies, he questioned them about the Romany language. He had some familiarity with it from George Borrow's books. Apparently they knew more French than Romany, but they did come up with *sap* ("snake"), *tud* ("milk"), and *Moldivus* ("Christmas"). Since that about exhausted Jim's vocabulary, they passed the test.

Mister Crow—who had been cruising about in the air, now disappearing over the hedgetop, now reappearing to bank against the cliffside—returned to settle on a nearby boulder and fix us with his black beady eye.

Here were these two people, parents of six children, the oldest of whom was nineteen. They'd lived together, presumably for twenty years or more—always, no doubt, on the go. They were obviously French gypsies: nothing Hungarian, Rumanian, or Middle European about them. Yet France doesn't like gypsies. Everywhere we'd seen signs warning gypsies that they were not wanted, that they could not camp, that they would be prosecuted if they did. Had this couple spent twenty fugitive years going from hideout to hideout, cut off from their own people, from all people?

"Where did you meet each other, at Les Trois Saintes Maries?" I was eager to show I knew about the annual conclave of gypsies near Marseilles.

"No, we were already married when we went there," she replied. Where they did meet, she kept to herself.

Jim courteously offered a few francs toward the forty thousand (or four hundred) they required, and she accepted them.

The man, as though it had something to do with the fact that she handled the exchequer, explained that she had *maladie de coeur* ("heart trouble"). (That was why she'd stashed away her cigarette, I thought. She was saving it for him.)

There was no sign of covered wagon, tent, or beds. In the open wagons were tumbled some dirty comforters. Scattered on the ground were a few pots and pans, and among the coals stood a small circular trivet, black with soot.

It was all pretty sordid.

But somehow that small black trivet, sitting low over the bed of smoking coals and ash, thrilled me to the core. It symbolized what I wanted to believe was a snug, romantic, anachronistic way of life.

Trying diplomatically to address myself to both, I asked if they would permit me to take a photograph or two.

"*Non,*" they replied in concert. No hesitation, no questioning looks exchanged, no two ways about it. Well, perhaps we hadn't given them enough money. People trying to raise forty thousand francs, or even four hundred. . . .

Jim offered to give them more *pour une seule photographie* ("for just one photograph"). In my mind I was composing the picture. How could I get the tame crow against a light background? Would I need the wide-angle lens to include all the wagons and the three bales of sweet-smelling hay that I had just now noticed? ("Stolen hay," Jim opined later, "stolen in advance, for the donkey they hoped to steal.")

But they were firm. *Pas de photographie.*

"*Eh bien,*" said Jim, and gave them another five francs anyway. His open hand was one of the many things I loved about him.

We wished them luck and squeezed through the thicket again, out onto the road.

All the way to our destination we puzzled and speculated. Had we offended them? How might we have won their confidence? Over dinner we talked and wondered some more. Like them, we were wanderers—rebels in our own way against conformity. Couldn't they have seen we were on their side? Surely they didn't fear any magic from the camera. They weren't savages. It was Jim's conviction that somehow they had taken us for agents of the law.

"You'll see. We'll go back there in the morning and there won't be a trace of them."

Another thing I always enjoyed about my husband was that not quite all his predictions came true. The gypsies were still there in the morning.

The woman was lying under a dirty blanket in one of the wagons; the wagon was tipped so that her head was lower than her feet. Had they heard us coming, as Jim argued later, and hustled her into the wagon to play on our sympathies, or was she really ailing, as I wanted to believe?

The man was sitting idly by the fire. Dog and crow as before. Six children as before, absent. Did the children really exist?

They were still talking of forty thousand francs.

Once more we offered additional francs—ten this time—for the privilege of taking a picture. Once more they declined. Were they holding out for still more? Should we have gone higher? After a little more talk we departed, no wiser. Friend crow looked as though he knew the answers to all our questions but wouldn't tell.

Somehow, though, we were richer. Not because they'd refused to have their picture taken, for we'd given them the extra ten francs anyway. Richer because we knew there were still real gypsies, people who could answer that *sap* means "snake," people who didn't care a fig for real estate, people who (dishonest, perhaps; dirty, incontestably) still had a certain *fierté*, a pride and self-esteem that are like the secret life at the heart of a seed.

I wish them luck. I often think of them: Where are they camped? Are those six children with them? Will they be going to the gypsy reunion in May? In what snug hideout have they built their latest fire and set over it that magical, soot-blackened trivet?

Why walking trips? People have always wanted to know. Because of gas prices? No, we started long before the oil embargo.

Wouldn't we cover more miles if we went by motorcycle? Covering miles was never our objective.

Isn't walking awfully tiresome? Tiring sometimes, but never tiresome.

Wouldn't we keep fit just as well in fewer hours by jogging? Let others jog. Walking is quite as healthful and a lot more fun. We never owned a car. We always walked a lot, and for the first thirty-four years of our married life, virtually the only medical expenses we had for ourselves were those of child bearing and checkups.

On summer walking trips we averaged at least seventy-five miles weekly, seeing the country better than do speedier travelers, remembering what we'd seen, and improving our French.

In our small way, we acted as ambassadors of goodwill, making friends with the French and the French Canadians, showing them that Americans too are capable of *politesse.*

And Jim, in no small way during twenty-two years, brought to hundreds of students in the Cedar Rapids adult night school a unique appreciation not just of the French language but of "Frenchness" itself.

These are some of the answers to "why walking trips?" But the number one answer is our gypsies, and a hundred other little encounters, a hundred other catches and turns that never would have happened had we been traveling any other way than on foot. *To let the unexpected happen to us!* On a walking trip you know that after the right foot it's the left, and vice versa. Beyond that anything can happen.

Of ten walking trips Jim and I made, the first three were early in our marriage during our childless years. Then came three more with both children. After those came one trip without Dave but with Eve, another on which Eve joined us for the last twelve days, and more recently two when we were again a twosome.

This book is about the three all-family walking trips and the trip when Eve was with us throughout.

PART I
An Ineffectual Ladder

MAMA'S PET IDEA

I WAS in a deep despairing rut of housewifely routine. I felt ready to burst.

"Let's take a walking trip this summer," I suggested.

"Don't be absurd," Jim replied. "You know we wouldn't leave the kids."

"No, I mean all of us."

"Binkie, you're mad. Eve would ruin it." Eve was six. You just don't take six year olds on walking trips. Even Dave, at ten, might present some problems.

But as the winter dragged on and I got more and more frantic for something to look forward to, it occurred to me to strike at Jim's vulnerable spot, his passion for the French language—a passion born when, at sixteen, he visited France with his mother. Now, some twenty-eight years later, he was making a living as a private tutor in creative writing and in French. The hours he spent teaching French he never thought of as "work."

So I proposed a walking trip in French Canada. Success came so easily I felt almost ashamed of my guile. Instead of "Eve would ruin it," it was, "You'll have to carry her most of the time, the way you do when we go anywhere around here." One thing he didn't enjoy was carrying things in his arms.

She weighed a good solid fifty-one pounds and had a great way of wriggling and sliding and having to be "hitched up." She knew how to dig her toes into the kidneys, into the spleen, into tender organs whose names I couldn't even guess. Nor was she above putting things down my neck. All in all, to carry Eve was to learn the meaning of repentance. Still. . . .

I'd been bitten bad. The three short walking trips Jim and I had had in California before the children were born had failed by far to satisfy my yen for adventure. I could wait no longer. I'd have advocated a family walking trip if Eve had weighed a hundred pounds.

And so through the spring we read books, wrote letters, sent for maps, talked it up to the children, and began to assemble our equipment.

Like the walking trips Jim and I had made alone, this trip was planned with the conviction it would be more fun if we relied on real beds in hotels and cabins along the way. To try to carry bedrolls for the four of us would have been to burden ourselves more than we were willing to do. Likewise, we counted on breakfasts and dinners cooked by someone else. We would carry food and water for during the day, and personal items. Our researches told us it was practical.

David, every inch his father's son, got almost as much fun out of selecting his knapsack and canteen, sharpening his pocketknife, "doping" his shoes, and gathering together his own little first aid kit in a lozenge box as he was to get out of the trip itself. His knapsack was packed weeks before school let out.

Eve was judged too young to carry either a knapsack or a canteen, but a thoughtful relative sent her a tiny box camera for which I made a blue denim case on an over-the-shoulder strap. This was her "gear" and we had great hopes it would help to keep her going by contributing to her sense of importance—if that needed any contributions. As things turned out, it also took some pretty fair pictures.

For everything that went wrong on that first family walking trip, I and I alone was to blame. The day we arrived in Quebec I foolhardily walked under a ladder. Not just a little ladder—a big one.

After a delightful ride in a horse drawn carriage, we headed for the Plains of Abraham to relax on the grass. Here in 1759 Wolfe had attacked. Here was fought the decisive battle which determined that the British flag was to fly over Quebec, indeed over what was to become Canada. Here both Wolfe and the defending French general, Montcalm, lost their lives. Below the bluff now, liners were steaming up and down the St. Lawrence.

Spying a flower she wanted, or an interesting rock, Eve started down the hill, tripped, fell headlong, slid, and took a couple of square inches of skin off her face.

I had plainly caused the catastrophe by walking under the ladder. Jim didn't mince words about it: any fool could have foreseen something of the sort.

So the next morning when four Iowans turned up at the Bassin Louise waterfront to board a tiny lumber schooner, the *Gaspé Nord*, they were already 25 percent battle scarred. But Eve bore her scabs bravely.

A good part of the twenty-four-hour voyage was spent playing jacks on the floor of the wee salon, for we had concluded that the weight of one small rubber ball and ten jacks could justifiably be added to the collective load we were carrying. Indeed, they might be indispensable.

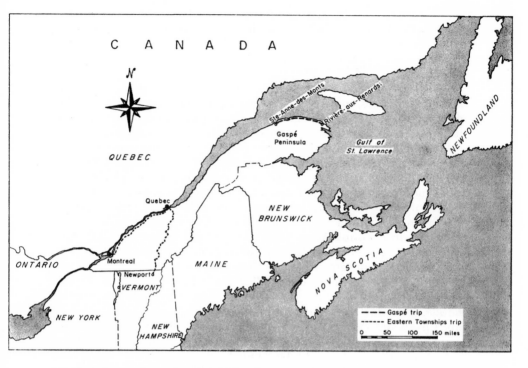

Bright and early the following morning we debarked at Ste-Anne-des-Monts, a tiny village with a mammoth church. Bundles of logs were already swinging up from the dock onto the deck of the *Gaspé Nord.*

From the foot of the gangplank we started our walking trip. It's a magical moment—that first stepping out; that severing of the last tie with the machine age; that renunciation of wheel, piston, and gear; that splendid gesture of independence. Your knapsack is on your back. You take a deep breath and simply start walking. You know you're going to get to your destination on your own.

Automatically we fell into line in the order we were accustomed to on day hikes at home in Iowa: Jim, then David, then Eve, then Mama.

By taking the steamer to Ste-Anne-des-Monts, we'd avoided the transition from the city of Quebec to the Gaspé Peninsula, being set down in typical Gaspésian territory. The interior of the peninsula is heavily wooded and virtually unpopulated. A necklace of small villages (many of no more than a hundred souls) runs around the coast, joined by a thread of blacktop. Each village is on its cove or *anse,* and into each *anse,* from the forested interior, flows a stream or *ruisseau.*

As we walked the blacktop, single file on the left side so as to face the traffic, the St. Lawrence was at our left, seldom more than half a mile distant, usually a lot closer. It was indeed the St. Lawrence but we couldn't see across it and we couldn't see any difference between it and an ocean. So we thought of it as "the ocean" and no harm resulted from this willful self-deception.

Between us and "the ocean" the land was under cultivation: potatoes, potatoes, potatoes. To our right the forest had in most places been cleared far enough to make another tier of fields. Beyond them rose the mysterious *montagne,* primitive and unknown.

In the fields were farmers who spoke to us in the curious, somewhat archaic French of Quebec Province. We both, especially Jim, delighted in noting the peculiarities of their accent and in theorizing about meanings, usages, and derivations. In some respects it was the French of Louis XIV with some quaint New World coinages added.

Eve did very well. Her legs, much the shortest, were nevertheless firm, sturdy pins. With her right in front of me, I could keep an eye on her; occasionally she walked at my side, holding my hand. Her tongue got almost as much mileage as her legs as she chattered about things at home. What really interested her most was: could she and Dave have a pet when they got home? Without delay the idea of a dog was whittled down to a provisional pair of miniature turtles—provided there wasn't too much bickering on the trip.

The very first day a scoring system was set up: at the end of each day each child would be graded on his behavior. If it had been satisfactory, a drawing of a turtle would be made in the square for that day. If less than satisfactory, the turtle would be minus an appropriate number of legs, or minus his head, or even bisected. Possibly, in extremis, just absent.

The system provided endless opportunities for exactly the kind of thing it was intended to discourage—taunts and teasing.

"Your turtle won't have any legs today."

"Well, you won't have any turtle at all."

I began to wonder whether my idea was, after all, inspired.

BAD LUCK AND MORE BAD LUCK

WE did about ten miles that first day and that turned out to be average for the trip.

While we were getting settled in a two-bedroom cabin at Ruisseau Castor (Beaver Creek) I walked from bedroom to bathroom, assuming, not illogically, that Gaspésian doorways were like other doorways. Most of them are. But this one was some eighteen inches lower than I had every reason to expect.

The thud brought Jim from one bedroom and the kids from the other. Since the comic-section days of my childhood I had wondered if people really saw stars after a blow on the head.

"I saw stars," I breathed. "I really saw stars."

My usually compassionate husband was applying cold compresses to my brow. He said nothing but there was clearly legible in his eyes the comment, "People who *will* walk under ladders. . . ."

Notwithstanding the lump on my forehead and Jim's expect-the-worst attitude, it seemed to me things were really getting off to a good start. Again the second day we covered our mileage. Huge trucks laden with monstrous logs careened around curves and down hills, only fanning us, never so much as scratching us. We found a cosy little beach upon which to have our lunch of sandwiches (made on the spot), milk (mixed on the spot, half water and half evaporated milk), fruit, and chocolate. The children played, hunted for shells, built sand castles and driftwood forts.

At our second overnight stop, Ruisseau Arbour, a malicious wind howled all night; the next morning it flailed and lashed around the cove so diligently that we decided to simply hole up in the cabin for another twenty-four hours.

As we left the main building after breakfast, the wind whipped a door out of our hands and slammed it against the building, shattering a large and expensive pane of glass. Jim proposed to the charming little proprietress that we should pay the damage.

"Ah non," she replied. "C'est du bad luck."

He regarded me silently, the "ladder look" in his eyes again. I began to feel like the fabled albatross.

It was July Fourth, a good day for a layover, and except for mealtimes we spent every minute of it in our one-room cabin, playing jacks and charades. Meanwhile, outside the wind raged on. If that body of water out there wasn't an ocean, how come it could work up such a storm?

The next few days went very well indeed. We were up in the morning and off soon after a breakfast of hot oatmeal with lots of

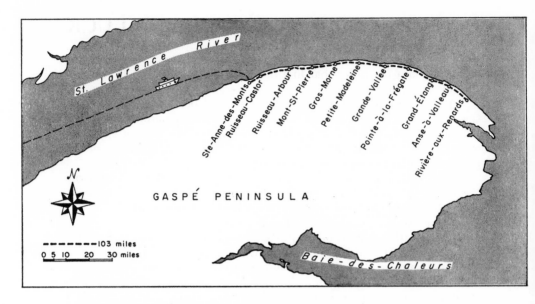

cream. On the road till late afternoon, we made frequent stops for snacks, for rests, for wading and playtime.

I learned to anticipate crossness and could sometimes head it off by suggesting a camera shot with the wee box camera. No suggestion was needed the day we encountered several boys with wooden-wheeled dogcarts drawn by great Newfoundlands.

Another way we had of alleviating Eve's boredom was singing songs and playing word games. When all the songs and all the games we could remember had been exhausted, we began again at the beginning.

The day we had to walk 14 miles to reach our destination took a lot of singing. For the last quarter mile I did relent and carry her. But of the full 103 miles, that was the only stretch that she didn't ambulate for her six-year-old self—a record to be proud of.

At the end of that fourteen-mile day we reached a charming country hotel on a rocky point, Pointe-à-la-Frégate (Frigate Point), where one of Gaspé's innumerable shipwrecks had occurred.

To travel the Gaspé Peninsula was to travel on an eternal Friday. Whether dinner was eaten in a hotel dining room or in a restaurant operated in connection with cabins, every night it was fish: salmon or cod, cod or salmon. And caught that day.

At forty-nine degrees north latitude in early July, daylight lingers until nine or ten at night. After dinner at Pointe-à-la-Frégate we went down to the beach to watch them hauling in the fishing dories.

On the rocky shore men and boys were turning crude capstans

whose cables were attached to the bows of high-gunwaled dories. Up out of the water the dories came, grating over the mess of rocks, broken shells, and seaweed. If that body of water wasn't an ocean, how come there was seaweed?

As the boats came to rest, tipping this way or that, the fishermen set to work at once, taking the fish out and cutting them on the tables that stood right there on the beach. Knives flashed; and fish heads, tails, and innards flew through the air to a pile on the rocks.

"I'm never going to eat fish again," Eve resolved.

"Then you'll go hungry in Gaspé," Jim kidded her.

"I don't care. It's too horrible."

David said he'd like to sneak a handful of the innards into Eve's bed.

"Mama, did you hear that?"

"There goes another leg off your turtle, Dave."

Now and again a man with a wheelbarrow would appear and haul away a load of the discarded parts. That explained why we kept smelling fish even when we were some distance from the river (ocean). They were using that piscatorial mess to fertilize their potato patches! It was eminently practical. Why should they pay for fish fertilizer when they had it on the beach for free?

Higher up on the beach were the "flakes" or drying tables with top surfaces made of chicken wire. During our ten days along the Gaspé coast, we saw thousands of fish spread out to dry on the flakes and many cylindrical piles of dried fish stacked about five feet tall and two-and-a-half feet in diameter. On such a pile was always laid a simple roof of birch bark to protect the dried fish from rain until the co-op truck stopped to make a pickup.

The hotel lobby at Pointe-à-la-Frégate was like a big family living room and at one end there was a small harmonium. To require children of six and ten to go upstairs to bed without having heard this instrument, strange and new to them, would have been a cruel and unusual punishment. The manager gave us permission to play the harmonium.

Jim sat down and began to pump the pedals. At perhaps the fourth stroke, there was a snap, a wheeze, and . . . silence. One of the straps from pedal to bellows had broken.

As I said, it wasn't just a small ladder. A safety pin got the thing working again, but it didn't get me out of the superstition doghouse.

BITTEN BUT NOT BEATEN

WE'D been on the road a week now. We were walking southeast, with an endless expanse of water to our left. Out of it the sun rose daily. The map told us it was still not the Atlantic but the St. Lawrence Gulf. Well, okay, the globe tells us the earth is round too. From where we were, the Gulf looked like an ocean.

We were observing that some diphthongs and ê's were pronounced as two separate syllables, as they had been in seventeenth-century France.

"Did you hear that, Binkie? She said *'shah-eez'* for *'chaise!'*" Sooner or later several other examples about which we had speculated turned up. One evening the choice of desserts included *"frah-eez" (fraises)* and *"pah-eesh" (pêches)*, and even the children chuckled. (A difficult choice it was too. The strawberries and the peaches were out of this world, second only to the *bleuets* ["blueberries"] which we had till we were *bleu* in the face but never tired of. And even the blueberries sometimes echoed strangely on the ear, for many of these people seemed unable or unwilling to pronounce a double consonant. *Bleuets* often came out *"beluets."*)

And yet the oi diphthong seemed to have gone the other way, and sometimes the ai as well. *"Il fah freh"* (for *il fait froid*), a farmer commented one chilly morning, though consistency would have called for *"il fah-ee froh-ee."*

Grand-Étang, our next overnight stop after Pointe-à-la-Frégate, turned out to be a great deception. In midafternoon the place appeared altogether charming. The village was, as its name implied, situated on a large pond—really the wide mouth of a stream nearly sealed off by a sandbar. We took a snug cabin with a view of the pond, rented a leaky rowboat, and set forth for some before-dinner fun.

The sun set and wham! The air was filled with mosquitoes the size of open umbrellas. In an endless succession of neatly executed passes, they whined in on us like kamikazes. If we scored hits on them, it counted for little. There were always more where they'd come from.

Hurriedly beaching our boat, we fled to the cabin. Alive with mosquitoes, it was humming like a peak-load dynamo. A token hand-washing and we made for the dining room. Surely it would be a secure sanctuary.

Not so. It was like a Roman arena. Evidently québecois blood had become tame and tasteless to the dainty mosquito palate. American blood was something gourmet. So the staff and the other guests, middle-class tourists from around the province, watched while the beasts devoured us outsiders.

We did manage to get some food into us, and that made a world of difference. In our family, a few calories could spell the difference between tragedy and comedy. We were soon laughing and joking just as though we didn't know a sleepless night awaited us.

As we dressed in the morning there was a stock taking.

"I've got six bites on just this one arm," David bragged.

"Look at this one," said Eve. "It's as big as a house."

I had a pair of bites close together that had blended into a huge welt which seemed to be unrivaled for size.

"Let's get dressed and get out of here," said Jim, scratching vigorously, "because I've just prayed that Grand-Étang will be swallowed up by a tidal wave."

It was our ninth setting-out-of-a-morning. In spite of mishaps and mosquitoes, we'd been having the time of our lives. In only eight days (some eighty-odd miles) we'd gotten so accustomed to the pattern of our new life that it seemed we'd been following that routine forever, that it was the normal and proper existence: up in the morning, hot oatmeal, knapsack packing, paying the bill, and setting off. We could count on the body of water somewhere off to the left, a body of land to the right, a suggestion of spray and fish smell in the air. We could count on being tired and hungry at day's end and on finding reasonable satisfaction for both. But otherwise what would the day be like?

Unforeseeable was the woman at a tiny general store and post office, who, when we asked to buy carrots, took us out back and dug them up—not from where they were growing but from where she had buried them to keep them from spoiling.

Unforeseeable the long roadside fence literally covered with caterpillars sunning themselves. We decided we couldn't wait around until they came forth butterflies.

Unforseeable the school of porpoises frolicking and leaping in the body of water as though expressly to divert the six year old whose legs were tiring.

Unforeseeable the hundreds of sprigs of evergreen stuck into the ground on both sides of the road to make a festive path for the statue of the Virgin being carried in procession from Cap-de-la-Madeleine six hundred miles away.

In just the right proportions, expected and unexpected had blended into a Gaspésian idyll. The paradox of a walking trip, repetitiousness coupled with constant change, had utterly enthralled me.

Just then, when (to me, at least) it had become like the breath of life, it was coming to an end. Time and money were running out.

From Anse-à-Valleau, where the bedsprings had stuck through, and the lemon wedges that came with our dinner fish had looked suspiciously as though we weren't the first to squeeze 'em, we set out on our last day's hike.

The children, it must be admitted, weren't sorry it was nearly over. Eve wanted not just drawings of turtles, she wanted turtles. Too, even at that age, she may have craved to wear a dress again. Dave, for whom even the novelty of building driftwood fires had worn off, wanted his pals on "the block" and baseball.

When Rivière-aux-Renards hove into view, we gasped (no pun) with unbelief at the billboard on the outskirts. It advertised a small hotel, and, wishing doubtless to convey "don't overlook us," it advised: Don't Stop Over.

We stopped over, nursed our mosquito bites, and wrote finis to our first family walking trip.

We may have thought we'd finished something. In truth, we'd just started something—something that walking under thirteen ladders couldn't spoil.

PART II
Bigger and Better

NORMANDY LANDING

THREE years, lacking a day, after stepping off the *Gaspé Nord* at Ste-Anne-des-Monts, we descended the gangplank of a Norwegian freighter at Le Havre to begin our second family walking trip. King size compared with the Gaspé jaunt (470 miles as against 103), it was simple and grand in concept. We were going to walk across France—just like that—from the English Channel to the German border.

As before, complete and ready, we were under way the moment our feet touched the shore.

Three years had made quite a difference. This time Eve, now nearly ten, was wearing a knapsack. Identical to mine, it was only a little less fully packed. In Gaspé I had carried her that quarter of a mile. By now, I couldn't have carried her twenty feet.

More thought and planning had gone into this affair, financially imprudent though it may have been. True, we had only a small-scale highway map of the country we proposed to traverse. That was naive. I was soon to learn that large-scale sections were indispensable. Otherwise, we'd thought of pretty nearly everything.

Heaviest items were several bottles of our favorite antiseptic mouthwash, unobtainable in France. A child's illness could have demolished our plan, and we were convinced a nightly gargle of the solution our pediatrician had recommended would ward off evil. Nice thing about that part of our load: day by day, little by little, it got lighter.

There were sweaters, jackets, changes of socks and underwear, raincoats, and first aid kit. For Eve and me I had tried in vain to buy suitable duck hats with brims and wound up making them myself. During 470 miles, Eve's hat in front of me reminded me that I was not to millinery born. The do-it-yourself *chapeaux* did, however, shade our faces.

There were four plastic glasses for the canned milk and water mix we'd drink during the day. The water would be commercially bottled spring water, decanted into the canteens. (Occasionally in a big city we filled our canteens right from the tap, knowing the water was safe.) We had a beer opener to pierce the milk cans, soap, elastic clothesline, sewing kit, and "haircut" scissors.

Of the unabridged *Les Miserables* in French, volume one was in my knapsack, volume two in Jim's. As usual he was one jump ahead of me. By now he was teaching French not only in our living room but in the adult night school.

Dave had his "squeezer," a spring contraption on which he was resolved to work out every evening to strengthen his already large and powerful hands.

As for Eve, the only distinctive item she had was a pair of red rubbers, and how she hated having to wear, from time to time, this double badge of humiliation!

There we were, on the continent of Europe with the whole of France stretching before us to the east. There was certainly no question about the body of water behind us. That was an ocean. For at least two weeks after landing, Jim was to insist he could still feel it heaving under him.

The first few days we followed the valley of the River Seine. It was fine Norman countryside such as we'd seen in travel folders, with poppy-spangled fields, thick-growing hedgerows, and thatch-roofed half-timbered farmhouses; with mammoth draft horses; with cows, pigs, ducks, geese, chickens, and rabbits; with chicory hanging up to dry; with roses and hollyhocks . . . an operetta countryside that looked as though it had never known war.

The people, mostly blond, weren't all as big as the Percheron-type blacksmith we saw shoeing a horse, but they were definitely not *petit*. Why, it was the Normans, of course! These French had Viking blood!

As we passed farm after farm and walked through village after village, it struck us that all the children were girls. They were fresh and healthy-looking girls, with rosy cheeks glowing above bright blue smocks. Some wore their hair bobbed, with bobby pins. Others wore it long. But where were the boys? The older ones might be working in the fields, but where were the little ones?

Then it dawned upon us: up to about age eleven, even the boys wore the blue smocks! They were the ones with the bobby pins. Then and there, Dave thanked his lucky stars he'd been born American. (This was, of course, before long hair for boys came to be "in.")

Single file and at the left of the road as in Gaspé, we kept to back roads as much as possible. As before, the standard order was: Daddy, Dave, Eve, Mama.

People raised their eyes from whatever they were doing in town or in the fields barely enough to size us up. They weren't the open, friendly, *accueillant* French we'd hoped for. Perhaps it was their Nordic blood.

As for the weather, we couldn't have planned it worse. This was the wettest summer in a century. The *potagers* that flaunted carrot, beet, onion, eggplant, parsley, lettuce, and cabbage in colorful array next to every dwelling were soggy mires. Fortunately even the back roads of France are mostly blacktop, so we had no need for *sabots*.

Our extra-large raincoats were worn over our knapsacks. What with Jim's bushy beard, his walking stick made from a rake handle, and the humps on our backs, we must have looked like four gnomes fresh from the Hall of the Mountain King. No wonder the French didn't run out and strew flowers! Between showers the sun came out —*un vrai soleil français*.

The first night we slept four in a room in a delightfully story-book *auberge*. In the night Eve, deciding she wanted to be close to Mama, got out of her bed and started crawling across Jim's to get to mine. Jim, half asleep, feeling something moving over him, and reasoning, storybook fashion, that we were beset by robbers and murderers, let out a yell that scared us all out of our wits.

Having disembarked with only a modest supply of French money, we were soon down to our last sous.

It hadn't surprised us that you can't cash a check just anywhere on a Sunday, the day we landed, but it did seem a bit hard lines that Monday too appeared to be a no-check-cashing day. Thus our initiation into the fact that in rural France, the banker, like the old American circuit-riding preacher, divides his time among several communities. La Remuée, where we tried to cash a travelers check on Monday, does all its banking when he comes on Tuesdays.

A kindly tavernkeeper was willing to take our last few French sous plus a stray American half-dollar one of us had. The big bottle of Norman cider he gave in exchange was well worth the trouble of dickering.

By and large though, people were not being too friendly, and it was taking the edge off our fun.

Then, like the case of the boys in blue smocks, it suddenly pene-trated. They were mistaking us for Germans! In French eyes, people walking with knapsacks on their backs just had to be Germans. Ego-tistically we had assumed they'd know it was English we were speak-ing among ourselves.

A small plastic American flag which I sewed to the flap of Jim's knapsack turned the trick. From then on they had nothing but smiles for us. They hadn't forgotten the Normandy landings, and we could now imagine how it must have felt to be Americans heading inland in 1944 through Normandy among a grateful people.

Our first few days there along the Seine inaugurated what was to be a long series of encounters with *épiciers* and *épicières*. Seldom a day goes by on such a trip that you don't stop in at a grocery store for a bit of chocolate, a couple of tomatoes, a bunch of bananas, a piece of cheese, or the like. We were to meet all kinds of grocery people—big and little, angry and gentle, primitive and cultivated.

Of them all, most charming was that little lady in Lillebonne, an *épicière* with the soul of a poet. She talked with us awhile about our trip. Then, her face suffused with a sublime radiance, she said, "Et le paysage est si beau!" and kissed her hand to the so-beautiful countryside.

Would that all patriotism were as pardonable. Unwittingly, she epitomized what General Charles de Gaulle was to say sometime later: Patriotism is when love of one's country comes first; nationalism is when hatred of other countries comes first.

It was our Lillebonne poet-grocer who told us to be on the lookout for the Victor Hugo house at Villequier, a riverside village we'd be passing through that day. She didn't know, of course, that Jim and I were reading *Les Miserables*.

The house, facing the river, was unmarked at that time but easy to identify from her description; likewise the little church where Hugo's wife Adèle and other members of his family are buried. Beyond the village a roadside marker commemorated the tragic death, in a boating accident on the river, of his daughter Leopoldine, only seven months after her marriage.

The following morning at Caudebec we were having *le petit déjeuner* of hot chocolate and fresh rolls with butter served in our room. The French doors were open onto a sunny balcony that overlooked the Seine.

The night before we'd seen a picture of the *mascaret*, or tidal bore, a wall of water which at high tide rushes up the Seine estuary—occasionally far up the river.

"I'd sure like to see that," Dave was saying. He was looking out at the river.

A moment later he let out a whoop, and naturally the rest of us assumed it was the *mascaret* he saw. But no. "It's the *Heina*, it's the *Heina!*"

Sure enough, steaming up the river past our hotel was the eight-thousand-ton Norwegian freighter that had been our home on the Atlantic for nine days. She was going up to Rouen to unload some cargo.

With lunatic cries, jumping up and down on the balcony and waving our napkins, we tried to attract the attention of the white specks on the bridge. They had other fish to fry, and we returned to breakfast.

It was the Fourth of July. Before setting out we found an illicit little shop that sold us some rather feeble miniature firecrackers.

At the bank, where we went to cash a travelers check, the teller was in some sort of international funk. Thinking dollars were pounds sterling, he gave us about four times as many francs as we were entitled to. Ah, sweet guilty moments—before honesty triumphed!

About noon, beside a deserted lane, there took place a minicelebration of American independence. For a family that has always been antiwar, we took a surprising pleasure in harmless explosions.

It was at Duclair that evening that we came face to face with the irreducible kernel of French hotel thinking. Duclair had borne some war damage. The hotel front was still in need of repairs. Across that front was a huge sign: *Demain la Façade, Aujourd'hui le Célèbre Caneton.* ("Tomorrow the façade, today the renowned [roast] duckling.")

The façade was indeed in dreadful shape. So was the rest of the building, outside and in. The sign itself was a bit the worse for wear. They had no intention of fixing the façade *demain* or any other day in the near future.

French hotels, we began to sense, had one room that mattered above all others, the *salle à manger.* The building could be a ruin, the walls peeling, ceilings stained, windows cracked, floors corrugated, furniture decrepit and tasteless, beds impossible. If the gastronomy was up to snuff, all was well. The French hotelkeeper catering to French travelers seemed well aware of this priority. So why should he indulge in façade repairs? Better to retain the handsomely paid chef whose roast duckling is celebrated.

After a dinner at which we studiously avoided that costly *célèbre caneton,* we rode a small auto ferry across the Seine and back, standing out on the diminutive apron to enjoy the breeze, the fading daylight, and the one-by-one-appearing lights along the riverfront.

It was good to be tired, to have satisfied our hunger, and to bob up and down on a famous river, catching now a bit of spray, now a wisp of smoke from the ferryman's cigarette, catching curiously clear fragments of song coming from a rowboat somewhere upstream.

A PRIZE SQUASH

BACK in our room at Duclair, I had strung up my elastic clothesline and was starting my nightly laundry chore when Jim reported that the bathtub plug was too big for the drain. He soon had the entire staff conducting a floor-by-floor, room-by-room search for one that would fit. In vain. Apparently no one ever used the bathtubs in this home of the celebrated roast duckling.

"Never mind." Out came Jim's knife. Presently he'd whittled down the oversize plug to fit, and water was trickling into the surprised tub. A maid stood by in wordless admiration of the resourceful, cleanliness-mad Yankees.

With four of us in one room, as we often were, it was amazing how long it could all take: baths, laundry, writing of diaries, sit-ups. (Yes! To have walked ten, twelve, fourteen, or more miles during the day wasn't enough. Dave did sit-ups every night, besides working out with his "squeezer.") Not to mention tending blisters. Plus the fact that dinner was seldom served before seven-thirty and was often a very lengthy affair.

So it was frequently midnight when our lights went out. But we were usually asleep ten minutes later—even Jim, who was an insomniac at home.

Our fifth day of walking brought us to what we'd determined would be our first layover place, Rouen.

The uses of an occasional layover are many. Laundry is paramount. A lesson learned in Gaspé had been: You can't wash a pair of slacks in a pint-size basin. Besides being on the lookout for generous basins, we'd gotten pretty astute at judging the truth of claims that there was *beaucoup d'eau chaude* ("plenty of hot water"). I'd developed a keen eye for hooks, hinges, knobs, and other protuberances that lent themselves to the stringing up of my clothesline.

There were shampoos on layovers, and, on that first long trip, there were usually shoe repairs for one or more of us. We were all wearing high (just above the anklebone) leather shoes with metal plates fore and aft. A good sleuth could have tracked us across France by those small crescent-shaped metal plates we kept losing.

Usually, too, on a layover day, there was sightseeing. Rouen was celebrating the five hundredth anniversary of the Rehabilitation of Eve's idol, Joan of Arc. The museum's special exhibition, impressive though it was, was less impressive than the small bare *cachot* where she spent her last night. Fresh flowers lay on the stone floor of the tiny cell; also on the slab marking the spot in the marketplace where she died among the flames, clutching an improvised cross handed her by an English soldier. We were all moved. For nine-year-old Eve, it was the first emotionally potent encounter with the reality of the past.

We refrained from comment on the irony of the Church's having "rehabilitated" Joan twenty-five years later and, several centuries after that, having canonized her.

We left Rouen refreshed. The only trouble was that as we left I spotted some luscious-looking marinated artichokes in the window of a *charcuterie*. They made a delicious gourmet roadside snack. But by midafternoon our little girl had a big tummyache. We stopped often for rests and strove with forced jollity to help her along.

About four o'clock we reached Fresne-le-Plan, our intended overnight stop, and my worst fears were confirmed. In plotting the itinerary, I had gambled on the rather small dot which represented Fresne-le-Plan on the map. I'd gambled there'd be some sort of inn. Fresne-le-Plan was a mere crossroads, a nothing. Perhaps they had a "plan" to make a village there but hadn't gotten around to it.

Our inquiries produced scant comfort: the nearest hotel was ten miles away. We could hire a car and driver to take us that ten miles. Or we could try to make it on our own.

It's easy to be gallant with other people's discomfort. Jim and I were sure Eve had nothing worse than a simple bellyache. We "helped" her decide.

"Do you feel up to walking a little farther, Evie?"

"Well, I don't know—"

"That's a good sport! It'll probably help you to feel better."

She was relieved of her knapsack; part of its contents going to Jim and Dave, the rest and the sack itself to me.

Like characters in some brave old pioneer story, we turned our backs on Fresne-le-Plan and hoped we could cover the ten miles to the alleged hotel in time for dinner and that there'd be beds for us.

We'd walked perhaps twenty feet when a car pulled up beside us, and what appeared to be a middle-aged, upper-class Frenchman spoke to us from the driver's seat.

"Voulez-vous m'accompagner à mon petit manoir pour prendre une tasse de thé?"

At four o'clock, with ten miles to walk, and a sick child—would we accompany him to his small manor to have a cup of tea? Time-wise it would be folly. But tea was just what Eve needed. We accepted invitation to tea, declined ride, and met him moments later at the *manoir*, where we sat at a delightful umbrella table in a charming garden and drank tea.

He wasn't a Frenchman at all but a retired English colonel who owned a textile mill near Rouen. He maintained a home in London, but preferred this second home, which he called Le Petit Manoir and, with his wife, spent most of his time here. She was away for a day or two. There was no trace of British accent in his French.

Our madcap idea of walking across France must have appealed to him for presently he invited us to stay for dinner and the night. We accepted with indecent alacrity.

Dinner, delicious, was served in elegant style by Colette, the pretty French girl who'd cooked it. By this time, tea, rest, kaopectate, and a highly selective dinner had about restored Eve, and there followed a pleasant evening listening to Colonel Mills's reminiscences of the war in North Africa—an evening as British as the Union Jack.

Colette treated us well. The next morning we repaid her by inadvertently locking her in her room. Her elaborate explanations after dinner about the layout of the upper floor and the use of the bathroom had fallen on weary ears. When once she was "sprung," she threw together a fragrant English breakfast—smelling which, we started downstairs.

It was a rather grand stairway, curved, with the individual steps very itsy-bitsy at the inside of the curve. Hungry Eve, weak from her ordeal, fell down the elegant stairway, breaking a mirror she carried in her pocket. Fortunately the Colonel had gone off to the races at Longchamps and did not witness her mishap.

So as we left Le Petit Manoir after that English breakfast, we had the one piece of equipment we'd lacked: a bad-luck omen, a broken mirror.

Again that day Eve's load was divided among us. It was a short day's lap, just eleven kilometers, part of it through fine beech forests.

The farther we progressed eastward, the more war monuments we saw, most of them decorated with fresh flowers. Coming into Lyons-la-Forêt, we noted the Stations of the Cross erected by the people in gratitude for having been spared the horrors of the German invasion. It made the war seem very real.

Gournay, the following night, was a market town still in process of rebuilding after severe bomb damage. But modernization hadn't gotten to Gournay's antebellum Hôtel de l'Agriculture, where Eve and I shared the world's narrowest double bed.

She had quite recovered from the artichoke affair, and beyond Gournay we took some long stages—thirty, thirty-one, and thirty-two kilometers (roughly nineteen, nineteen-and-a-half, and twenty miles).

Here in the old province of Ile-de-France, the forests with their tall beeches and spreading oaks appeared to have changed little since the days when they were royal hunting preserves. Now and then a woodcutter would look up from his work and soberly return our greeting. A sign warning that there might be *sangliers* just off the road put a pleasant tingle in our spines. I walked with my camera at the ready, but these wild boars didn't materialize. Next best, their hairy, tusky, ferocious heads glared at us, stuffed, from the walls of more than one cafe. "We may yet be glad I have this stick with the metal point on the end," Jim remarked with relish.

That we'd left Normandy with its Viking types was evident in Beauvais where the people were small, wiry, and swift of foot, hand, and tongue. They resembled the Parisians, and their city was like a vest-pocket Paris.

Somewhere on one of these better-than-thirty-kilometer days, I did something to my left leg. Either I got into some kind of poisonous vegetation or I pulled muscles, tendons, ligaments, or what-had-I. Anyway, my leg turned lemon yellow and swelled up like a prize banana squash. I managed to conceal it the first day, but it was finally discovered.

As usual in such a case, Jim was torn between real concern and thoroughgoing disgust. Every step was painful to me, and he was genuinely worried and sympathetic. On the other hand, no one but a fool would have a yellow leg! Doubtless it was the broken mirror.

Until now we had managed to stay on back roads. Paris was not in our plans for the walking trip. We would go there after we'd reached Strasbourg on foot. But we had come into the Paris orbit, and on the third of these long days there was no alternative but to do the whole distance on a main east-west highway, north of the capital. Heavy traffic didn't help matters. By the time we reached Compiègne we were all tired and cross. My leg was giving me real pain.

Believing we had the entire spread of a big city to cross in order to reach our hotel, we stopped at a sidewalk cafe. Jim and I each had a drink of calvados, a delicious, potent apple brandy, and the kids had some of their favorite orange drink. Thus fortified, we made it to the hotel—a scant two blocks away. For two days Compiègne was host to that great yellow leg.

MAMA ACQUIRES A MAJOR KEY

EVE and I beguiled a good deal of the time at Compiègne playing Battleships, a game of wits learned on the Norwegian freighter.

The first layover day there was July 14. Jim and Dave went to the Bastille Day shooting gallery where they spent twenty-four francs for turns and came back with two bottles of wine they'd won. Jim reckoned their retail value at exactly twelve francs each.

Leg elevated, I made a good deal of headway with *Les Miserables*.

On the second evening we attended our first *Son et Lumière* performance at the Chateau of Compiègne. Chairs were not provided. A few of the audience had brought their own folding chairs, some had spread blankets on the lawn, but most, ourselves included, simply sat on the grass facing the chateau, with backs to the long avenue cutting into the forest. Daylight was fading when the performance started, and the chateau was in sharp silhouette against the sky.

One by one lights came on in different rooms of the chateau, and recorded voices (of some of France's finest actors and actresses) were heard in narration and dialogue recounting historic happenings at Compiègne. Now the sound track would come from the garden where a lord and lady were having a clandestine meeting, and a spotlight would shine on the clump of shrubbery where they were supposed to be in tête-à-tête. Then perhaps back to the chateau, back to an upstairs boudoir where the young queen was writing in her diary, telling us what she was writing and letting us hear even the scratching of her quill pen. Then perhaps a ball, with the many tall downstairs windows ablaze with light, and music of the period. It was vividly real, all without our seeing a single human being.

We'd walked 248 kilometers (about 155 miles) in a couple of weeks. Except for that lemon—my leg—and a few blisters, we were in excellent shape. Jim was in high spirits because at long last the carryover pitch and roll of the freighter had left him. He was finally sure we were on terra firma.

There was no shadow of doubt in our minds that we could accomplish what we'd set out to do—walk across France. Determined to finish, come what might, we were also sure that several "whats" would come.

If only we could stay exclusively on back roads! By now I had acquired large scale maps, so I knew where the back roads were and how much mileage they would add. Most of the time we could stay on them, but sometimes in order to reach accommodations we had to settle for a bit of highway. Trespass on private property we would not.

Fresne-le-Plan was our last gamble on the existence of hotel or inn ahead. Even the pitfalls of making reservations via the French phone system were preferable to finding ourselves bedless. Thenceforth we were always booked ahead for accommodations.

I wished that at least a few of the "hotels and inns" would call themselves *auberges,* for that was what they were. But the truth is that except for the first night off the ship we neither stayed in nor saw anything bearing the magic name *auberge.* This was bitter fare for me, who had carried away from my schooling the image of half-timbered, thatch-roofed hostelries with fires in fireplaces, cats on hearths and above all, quaintly lettered signs saying *Auberge.* I wanted my *auberges!* I despise any French word that's spelled the same in English, even if its origin is clearly French. But they called themselves *hôtels,* not *auberges,* and we had no choice but to stay in them.

The raincoats and those red rubbers of Eve's worked long hours in the Forest of Compiègne, where, the next day we visited the famous Armistice car.

In virtually all the villages we'd passed through, there'd been those monuments to the war dead with their long lists of names, often with fresh flowers at the foot. In one place, ashes. There'd been the towns like Gournay, still repairing or replacing their war-damaged buildings. There'd been the red circles on my up-to-date maps—circles indicating "bridge out" or "bombed area."

Now in the Forest of Compiègne we entered the railroad car where the 1918 Armistice was signed . . . saw the pens with which signatures were affixed, the chairs in which signers sat, facsimiles, clippings, mementos pertaining to the *Waffenstillstand* . . . saw the stereopticon pictures from all battlefronts in all their frightful three-dimensional realism . . . tried somehow to convey to the children a sense of what it meant . . . stepped out into the rain again, wondering whether swords will ever finally, forever, be beaten into plowshares.

Compiègne was only a third of the way across France. There were to be more bombed cities rebuilding from World War II. There were to be military cemeteries with their ranks of white crosses receding into the distance. There were to be monuments commemorating atrocious acts by the Nazis. And everywhere the inescapable monuments in village squares: "1914–18" on one side and on the other "1939–45." On the lists of dead were the same family names we were seeing as we walked along through village and countryside. The dates of birth and death . . . so many dead so young.

Thoughtlessly planning our walking trip across northern France, we hadn't reckoned on daily reminders of two World Wars. We had come to France to have a good time, to speak the language, to enjoy the people. In general we were doing it. Yet there were periods when the adults in our little party walked along wrapped in somber thought.

There were things to be joyous about too. The weather cleared briefly. The people, now that they could see we were Americans, were friendly. While many villas had dogs advertised on the gate as *méchant*, none of them had bitten us. Visiting an historic stone abbey, we learned that the roof had fallen in three weeks before. It could well have waited and fallen on us.

On a run-of-the-mill day our knapsacks carried bread or crackers, sausage, canned milk, fruit, and chocolate. The episode of the artichokes had taught me nothing about the folly of trying to vary what was a perfectly satisfactory arrangement. I wanted to experiment.

One day I decided to get sardines instead of sausage. Seated in the shade of a couple of handsome poplars and all four primed for a delicious snack, we discovered the can was lacking a key. Out came Dave's Boy Scout knife. In all other respects an admirable tool, it was a fraud as a can opener. Eventually we got a small jagged corner pried up enough to torture a few scraps of fish out, and by the time the snack was over, my slacks were surrealist with oil.

Some days later I bought more sardines. "Une clef, s'il vous plaît, monsieur," I demanded.

"Oui, madame," and he dropped a key quickly into the sack.

Some ten kilometers on, the key was found to be the wrong size. Another case for the Scout knife.

Again I bought sardines.

Me: "Et une clef, s'il vous plaît, monsieur."

He: "Je n'en ai pas, madame," with that helpless French shrug of the shoulders. He had no keys. "Mais vous pouvez en acheter en face." (I could buy one across the street.)

I still have the key I bought at that hardware store. It measures a medieval seven inches and weighs as many ounces. It's a key in whose company I wouldn't be afraid to go anywhere at night.

CHAMPAGNE FIND

THE Abbaye St-Jean-des-Vignes at Soissons did not have its name for nothing. We were getting into the wine country. Reims (Rheims) was only two days distant.

Mere mention of a French vineyard conjures up an idyll: ancient gnarled rootstocks, shapely green leaves, purple grapes heavy with juice, vines marching in fine straight rows up the hillside, and the whole bucolic scene bathed in golden sunlight.

But on the second of the two days between Soissons and Reims, where Saint John of the Vines ought to have been keeping an eye on things, things were not idyllic. The vineyards we passed were drenched in rain, the same rain that was compelling us to walk in those hot, sticky raincoats.

Dave, who till now had never shown any sign of fatigue or weakness, proved to be human. A neglected blister on his big toe had become badly infected. Jim's rough way of "operating" sometimes led the children and me to hide our injuries for fear of the treatment, but on this occasion even Dave's Spartan hardihood could not conceal a limp.

At the moment it wasn't raining. We all sat down at the side of the road, and Jim disinfected and bandaged the toe while Dave, who possessed a merit badge in first aid, told him bluntly that in rendering first aid a Boy Scout is "not only efficient but gentle and considerate."

It was to be a thirty-kilometer day (about nineteen miles). Eve had bravely done her digestive suffering. I had borne my banana-

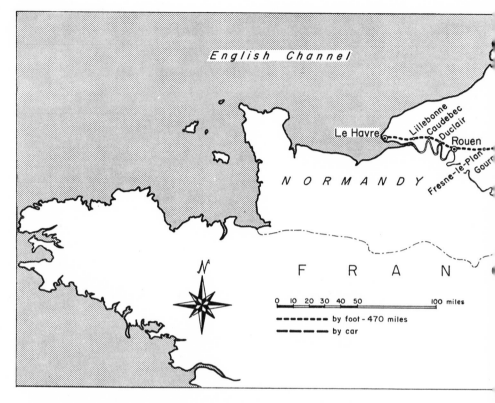

squash *jambe jaune*. It was Dave's turn for martrydom. He insisted the toe was not hurting him, though from my spot at the end of the line I could see him limp with every step and knew he lied.

There was plenty of penicillin ointment in the first aid kit, and we kept close watch for the red streak that would warn of blood poisoning. The show went on (though we were our only audience) and we reached Reims as planned.

A layover was scheduled there. There was mail to pick up, laundry to be done of course, clothes to be mended, haircuts to be given, film to be bought, shoes to be taken for repairs. There was the cathedral where Jeanne d'Arc had crowned the Dauphin. There were the 250 steps to climb in one of its towers for a superb view from a gallery near the top. There were the renowned champagne cellars.

Singly and in pairs Jim and Eve and I were busy, were in and out. But for two days Dave just took antibiotics and stayed off his toe. Gradually the infection responded.

A discouragement had taken hold of us. Try as I would, I could not seem to figure out a route that would get us where we wanted to go (Strasbourg), provide us with fair accommodations en route, and

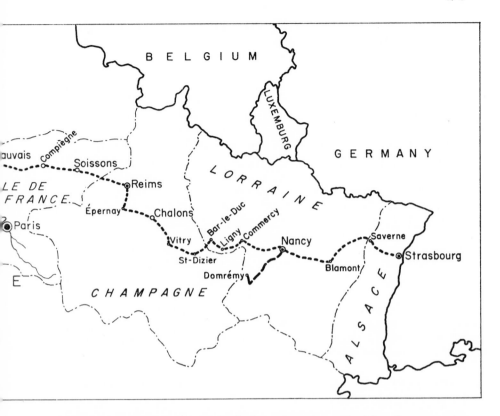

keep us on back roads. It looked as though we'd either have to give up our idea of an uninterrupted trans-France walk or resign ourselves to a good many days on the highway, with cars zooming past at frightening speeds, with noise and nerves for all. To give up was out of the question. After a two-day layover we left Reims, resigned to doing the last half of our walk mostly on the highway.

This was the province of Champagne. Champagne vineyards lay before us, behind us, around us. We would enjoy ourselves if it killed us!

"Champagne to our real friends," I said, quoting my Lorrainer great-aunt.

"Real pain to our sham friends," finished Jim, who knew the great-aunt's sayings as well as I did.

There was the bridge over the Vesle River, then another over the Aisne-Marne Canal, busy with barges. A rosy, well-endowed bargeman's wife came ashore with a big galvanized pitcher and put it under a tap near the lock. As it filled, she stood talking with the lockkeeper's wife who sat on a bench knitting. Across the canal a housewife of Reims sat on a stool, likewise knitting, while she kept an eye on her black goat as he grazed on public grass.

It was typical of the waste-not–want-not of France. Odd moments, like odd patches of earth and grass, like odd sticks and twigs, all are put to use. If a person raised rabbits, he kept them in a bottomless cage which was moved systematically from place to place so they would crop the grass evenly. If a lot was irregular in shape, so was the vegetable garden. If one went to pay a condolence call, one took along a string bag and filled it with dandelion greens on the way home. And as much knitting and sewing as possible was done outdoors to save electricity.

Not that this was poor country. Beyond Reims it was very prosperous. And why shouldn't it be, with champagne at a dollar a glass and tourists willing and eager to pay it? The vineyards, growing in their famed chalk soil, were luxuriant, scientific, endless.

After walking all morning long, we could still see the great cathedral back at Reims.

The fact that, instead of stopping for a real midday meal, we made only brief snack stops at irregular intervals took some of the curse off having to follow the highway along here. The French seemed to regard the noon meal as sacred. Vacationers would call a halt at some hotel or restaurant and order a full *déjeuner*. Or they'd pull off at the roadside, conjure up out of the car trunk a table, chairs, napery, china, wineglasses, utensils, and a huge hamper of goodies: solid, semisolid, liquid. There they'd sit over a four-course meal, for all the world as though at home in the *salle à manger*—yet just five fork-lengths from the passing traffic.

A pleasant sight was always the big family reunion at some *café champêtre* ("country cafe"). Near Champillon we observed one such, made up of perhaps two dozen individuals of three or four generations. Their dress and behavior were ambiguous. Was it a wedding party? A postchristening celebration? A funeral lunch? We dared not ask.

Even traveling salesmen and truck drivers would observe the lengthy break, sitting in car or cab to replenish calories and then leaning back for forty winks.

The noontime lull was our salvation, a respite from the whizzing vehicles that sometimes came so close they blew our hats off.

We weren't meeting long-distance walkers like ourselves, but often every day we encountered farmers and their families on foot between village and field. Officialdom was mindful of them, cautioning them from walls everywhere. *Marchez à Gauche,* said the posters, *Face au Danger.* ("Walk on the left, facing the danger.") That was what we'd been doing all along. At the head of the line, Jim watched the oncoming cars for dangerous passing, and at the tail end I did likewise to the rear, looking over my shoulder often and listening always for menacing sounds. At the least threat of danger from either direction, one of us would shout "Over!" and all four would leap off into the ditch or up the bank. Jim's and my tension was equaled by the children's annoyance at having their conversation or thoughts constantly interrupted.

All this took some of the bloom off the dreamlike "Italian hills" views that opened out from summits here and there, but it couldn't spoil them altogether.

At last, after twenty-seven kilometers, we set foot in Épernay, another renowned champagne center. Strasbourg was one day closer.

Across the river from Épernay the next morning, at the unlikely village of Aÿ, we encountered the Marne Canal, and I wistfully remarked that according to the map this canal went all the way to Strasbourg.

Eve looked down from the bridge by which we were crossing and commented, "There's a nice path alongside it."

It was like when the pinball machine goes wild, with bells ringing and lights flashing. An idea was born. Quickly we consulted the lockkeeper, who told us *oui*, the canal went clear to Strasbourg, and *oui*, there was a towpath all the way. And the command "Over!" dropped from our vocabulary.

IN FULSOME PRAISE
OF WATERWAYS

CANALS were known in many parts of the ancient world but fell into disrepair and disuse after the decline of the Roman Empire. The canal with locks, the modern concept of canal, dates from about the fourteenth century in both Europe and the Orient. It is far from being an exclusive possession of France. Look at England: what would *The Wind in the Willows* be without Mr. Toad's outrageous adventures on the canal?

But it seemed to us that inland waterways are something for which the French have a special feeling, as they have, for example, for wines, cheeses, perfumes. The poet Baudelaire was alive to the magic of canals and their barges when he wrote *L'Invitation au voyage*.

After our return home I tried, by translating part of the poem, to capture some of the elusive beauty of his lines:

> See how on these canals
> Sleeping vessels lie—
> Things of vagabond spirit.
> To satisfy your least desire
> They come from the ends of the earth.
>
> Setting suns clothe field,
> Canal, and town complete,
> In hyacinth and gold;
> And, in a warm glow,
> The world goes to sleep.
>
> Naught there but order and beauty,
> Ease, calm, delight.

There are some three thousand miles of canals in France, linking up thousands of miles of navigable rivers and even linking ocean to ocean. French canals date mostly from the eighteenth and nineteenth centuries. As early as the seventeenth century an important one was built by an obscure tax collector, Pierre-Paul Riquet. He constructed the Canal du Midi to link Atlantic and Mediterranean, bypass Gibraltar, and thus do the King of Spain out of some taxes.

Many of the canals have towpaths where horses used to plod, paths made to order for people like us. We saw an occasional diesel tractor chugging along the path with a barge in tow, as well as electric tractors that ran on tracks. There were also a few barges being pulled or pushed by tugs. But commonest by far were the barges with their own engines. Now there's a life!

She's about 125 feet long, this average barge, and about 16 feet wide. She draws 8 to 10 feet of water. She has for crew—the family. Once the holds are filled with, say, three hundred tons of grain or oil from some ocean-goer at almost any West European port, the long voyage begins, first up river, then by canal perhaps to another river, and very likely across frontiers. Canals and/or navigable rivers link France with Belgium, Holland, Germany, Luxembourg, and Switzerland.

Both bargeman and spouse take spells at the tiller. Snug quarters are aft, below decks. Cooking, washing, and ironing are done as at home. In fact, it is home.

By the time two or three of the barges had passed us as we walked along the quiet towpath, we were resolving to spend our old age in this fashion.

Whole families live on these unbeautiful craft. What a heartening sight it is to see one come round the bend with its flag flying, a barking dog running along the gunwales, bright geraniums blooming in pots by the galley, baby creeping in a playpen, and from stem to stern a line of diapers flapping white and free in the breeze!

On Sundays we'd see barge families taking their ease after a picnic on shore, lying on the grass, reading the paper, or even taking a dip in the canal.

For practical reasons we didn't follow the Marne Canal all the way to Strasbourg. But we did follow it and other canals a good many of the remaining fourteen days of our Channel-to-Rhine walk—enough so that the prevailing atmosphere, instead of being that of the highway with its traffic and tension, was incredibly peaceful.

Where, for purposes of gradient, the canal had been cut into a hill, it might be that all we could see over the banks would be a row of treetops, a few tile roofs, a church steeple, the tiptop of a haystack. Where, for the same reason, it ran on the flat or on a built-up embankment, we could see a broad sweep of French countryside.

Always we enjoyed a sense of unequaled peace and privacy. It was hard to believe that there were some ten thousand barges constantly plying the inland waterways of France, transporting nearly ninety million tons of cargo every year. We saw so relatively few of them.

On the stretches where towing was by electric tractor, the tracks were on one bank only, and we took the other.

Both the "dumb" barges (those being towed) and those with their own diesel motors moved quietly and slowly—not more than seven or eight miles an hour. Anything faster than that tends to break down the banks, which, even so, have to be protected here and there with corrugated iron sheets driven into the earth. Prettier by far than those rusty sheets were the rushes planted next to the banks to absorb and reduce the lapping action of the wakes. In among these the waterbirds had their nests, and from out of them they came winging low, skimming the water.

Now and then a dredge would come along, deepening the channel. Occasionally there'd be a man with a scythe, trimming the growth on the bank of a turn, so bargemen could see ahead.

From time to time there'd be a fisherman staring contentedly at the green water, his two or three rods held in place with forked sticks so that he could instantly tend them if fortune struck, which it seldom seemed to do. Beside him his wine bottle, his bread and sausage.

Of course the canals went through the bigger towns. There the barges loaded and unloaded freight. This circumstance sometimes brought us excellent accommodations, all the conveniences. The canals sometimes went through or passed small villages at a distance of less than a kilometer. In the former case there might be a cafe at the water's edge, just when we were in the mood for cool refreshment. In the latter case we could take off for the village cafe and then return to the towpath to go on.

At intervals of as little as a kilometer and a half or as great as four or five kilometers, there were locks, usually in pairs so that barges going in opposite directions could be accommodated simultaneously. Most of the basins were big enough to take a couple of barges at a time, or a barge and a tug, or a barge and a pleasure boat. The rise and drop was 8 to 12 feet.

It was a delight to see a long barge with its three hundred to a thousand or more tons of cargo move cautiously into place in a lock and then to watch the huge gates close behind it in obedience to a simple handcrank turned by some aged lockkeeper or his none-too-robust wife or perhaps their little grandson. Simple demonstrations of basic mechanical principles like this always thrill my naive mind. Had I been present at the invention of the wheel, I would have swooned.

To me the locks were great engineering triumphs. There were greater wonders, though. There were places where canals crossed roads, passing above them; places where they passed above a railroad and at the same time under a highway; places where one canal crossed another, one passing over the other. You name it—*messieurs les ingénieurs* had devised a way to do it.

There are even places in France where canals go through tunnels. It was well we didn't happen on any of them, because for some reason (perhaps they feared the horses would shy) no towpaths were provided in these tunnels. In the days before powered barges, there were three methods of getting the craft through tunnels: they were pulled through by an endless chain; they were poled through by bargemen walking along the gunwales; or they were "legged" through —bargemen, lying on the hatches, "walked" on the tunnel walls. That's a sight I'd give a lot to have seen! Slavery, serfdom, Volga boatmen, men on treadmills—no, I draw the line. But free men driving their own barges through tunnels by walking on walls! Sometimes I lie awake at night imagining it.

BIRTHDAY WITH A TWIST

THE barges were not strangers to us. Before docking at Le Havre, our Norwegian freighter had made a four-day call at Antwerp. It was a rainy four days and a good part of our time there had been spent hanging over the railing in a mild hypnosis, watching huge suction pipes transfer American grain from our hold into the holds of barges. One bargeman had become our friend.

Most foreigners who pass through Antwerp or any other European harbor linger at most a day or so in the city, not at all on board ship. It was, for this bargeman and his wife, an unusual chance to talk with Americans. The couple had shown a lively interest in us, the children, and our delirious plan to walk across France.

When the hold was filled, they battened down their hatches and chugged away in the drizzle. No doubt such a departure is usually quite unnoticed by anyone once the necessary business forms are completed. But a certain élan was conferred upon this departure by the four Americans standing at the railing of the *Heina,* waving and nodding and calling out their *au revoirs.*

So now, about four weeks later, walking the towpath on the day that we discovered the canal to Strasbourg, we regarded all bargemen and their families as our distant cousins.

Late in the afternoon a barge appeared, coming toward us at some distance.

"That barge hath a familiar look," said I. What was familiar about it? I don't know. My comment was one of those spontaneous, intuitive remarks that occasionally rise to the surface and just spill from one's lips as though directed by some separate intelligence.

"It's the *Pampero!*" cried Jim. Back at Antwerp the name had struck him—Argentina and the pampas being so far away.

Sure enough, it was our friend and he remembered us. The *Pampero* had come up the Albert Canal, the rivers Meuse, Sambre, and Aisne, and the Aisne-Marne Canal. "Viens, viens vite!" he called below decks. Up came his wife and the dog, the latter almost beside himself with excitement at recognizing us. There was just time for a few disjointed greetings and then they were out of earshot, their voices muffled by the chug-chug of the diesel motor. They and we continued waving a long time.

At Aigny, somewhere along the Marne Canal, a deaf old woman, shouting a double forte, recounted to us the tale of how, during the first World War, she had served a beer to an American colonel on a Tuesday in November 1918, and how he had told her there'd be an armistice soon and it came the following Monday.

She apparently felt that this (to her, occult) happening was her most significant and tell-worthy experience of two World Wars. She had surely seen war's weariness, filth, disfigurement, and death, but this narrative seemed to give her the sense of drama and importance her ego demanded.

As we approached Châlons-sur-Marne, footsore after more than thirty-three kilometers, we were joined by a Récy farmer returning to town after the day's work in his field. He had something to tell that was a bit more hair raising than the old woman's anecdote of the prescient beer drinker. During World War II a Royal Canadian Air Force plane had come down in flames in the very field he was now returning from, and he had pulled a crew member from the blazing wreckage and, assisted by his wife, had hidden and cared for him. The couple had received *des diplômes* from the French government for their assistance to this flyer and other Allied troops. This man was no braggart. He was simply recounting to four Americans an experience that he felt was part of the common stream of Allied history.

David's toe was still not a pretty sight, and, over his protests, we took another layover at Châlons. It gave us a chance for needed shoe repairs, for a third-rate movie, and best of all for wandering around —the three of us who could afford more mileage—in the place where, more than five centuries before, Jeanne d'Arc had spent two nights on her way to Reims to crown the Dauphin.

Too, it gave me time to commune still further with maps and my hotel guide. Between us and Strasbourg on the Rhine lay something more than two hundred miles. I was determined: (1) to plot as much of it as possible along the canals, (2) to bring us to roost each night in some fairly decent nest, and (3) to see to it that somewhere along the line, since it wasn't going to be possible to walk to Domrémy, we should at least manage a side trip by bus or car to Jeanne d'Arc's birthplace. Emerging from my researches, I was confident of success in (1) and (3). About (2), only time would tell.

My mumblings and mutterings of village names as I pored over the maps inspired Dave, whose silly streak always broadened during periods of forced inactivity, to discover what would prove a rich vein of humor over the remaining two hundred miles. He suddenly decided the French language was funny—especially French place names. The improbable combinations of letters with their still more improbable pronunciations tickled his funny bone till he doubled up with mirth. That a little feeling for the language was seeping in, however, was evident a day or two later when he uttered his immortal do-it-yourself version of "live and learn": "Nous libre que nous lerne."

Only once and only very briefly in the twenty miles from Châlons to Vitry did we have to leave the Marne Canal.

From Vitry, a town that appeared to be completely new—entirely rebuilt after war damage—to St-Dizier, we were following the Marne-Saône Canal, narrower and on the stagnant side. Here and there the avenues of poplars that lined it were heavily draped with mistletoe. Frogs boomed among the rushes. Cattle grazed in the fields beside the canal. Everywhere near human habitation were flowers, flowers, flowers.

Hot and thirsty at one point, we rejoiced to see a farmhouse displaying the familiar red lozenge, *la carotte.* This symbol is derived from the shape of the plugs in which, in the early seventeenth century, tobacco was sold, to be grated for snuff taking. It often indicates a place where, in addition to tobacco products, drinks can be had, both hard and soft. In this case other clues were absent, but our intuition proved correct. The farmhouse was indeed a cafe— a cafe of which chickens had free run.

Le papa seated us in the kitchen and dispatched *le petit* for *la maman,* who came in from the barn and, with debonair disregard for sanitation (an attitude fortunately now on the wane) proceeded to serve us without so much as wiping, much less washing, her capable hands. That we survived our long walk across France was perhaps less a tribute to our pedal fortitude than our intestinal ditto.

During the last few kilometers before St-Dizier we had the pleasure of paralleling the highway. Within sight and sound of traffic zooming along fast and furiously, we trod our quiet towpath accompanied by a small bird who flew ahead of us, perched on a branch, let us pass him, once more flew ahead of us, and so on indefinitely. Off in a field were a couple of gypsy caravans. Perhaps those people shared our sense of privacy and privilege.

It was July 28, the date we habitually celebrated as "Ouray's birthday"—Ouray being the survivor of the pair of turtles awarded at the end of the Gaspé trip. Ouray was safe at home in the care of a playmate. Some observance of his birthday was called for, and the menu at St-Dizier that night provided the answer: we had turtle soup for dinner. A twisted way to celebrate? Perhaps, but it was delicious.

A GOOD QUESTION

EVE'S birthday, which followed immediately upon that of Ouray, was celebrated with a day's layover. She was turning ten. She was not the same girl she'd been three years before in Gaspé. More was expected of her. She walked farther, carried more, complained seldom, and bore her big brother's taunts more calmly.

If she began to tire at the end of a long day, she could always be humored by thoughts of the dinner that awaited. Jim made up new words to be sung to the tune of "Frère Jacques":

> Mon potage, mon potage,
> Que je t'aime, que je t'aime!
> Donnez-moi ma cuillère,
> Donnez-moi ma cuillère!
> J'ai grand faim,
> J'ai grand faim!

In English it was:

> My soup, my soup,
> How I love you, how I love you!
> Give me my spoon,
> Give me my spoon!
> I'm very hungry,
> I'm very hungry!

What the natives thought, if any heard us singing this version of their old standard, we'll never know.

Nor shall we know what they made of Dave's teasing "She braids through thick and thin." Eve had recently learned to braid, and often walked along braiding grass.

That both kids were physically tougher than in Gaspé was brought home to us from time to time when, after a long hard day, they would tear around the hotel room like fresh young colts, romping and playing, while their wilted parents caught a few minutes' lie-down before dinner.

As we left St-Dizier, we found ourselves walking behind a funeral procession. Drawn by horses wearing black blankets, the hearse crept slowly out of town toward the cemetery. The pallbearers walked beside it and behind it, each one holding the end of a wide black streamer that was attached to the coffin. Mourners, young and old, in black from top to toe, walked behind, singly and in pairs.

The moment we realized what was happening, we stepped off

the road and allowed the cortege to get some distance ahead. With our knapsacks, canteens, homemade hats, and informal attire, we would have added a grotesque note indeed.

Ten kilometers out from St-Dizier, we left the province of Champagne and entered Lorraine. Being beyond the orbit of Paris and taking to the highway only briefly, we found the traffic bearable.

At Brillon a statue of Napoleon on a pedestal caught our eye. Statues of the Emperor had been conspicuous by their absence. Post–World War II Frenchmen seemed content, on the whole, to forget the Napoleonic chapter of their history. Even Brillon was rather timid about acknowledging that troublesome Corsican, for the Emperor's statue stood no more than eighteen inches high.

Presently we were in the orbit of the U.S. Army, for there was an American ordnance depot at Trémont-Trois-Fontaines. Jeeps, trucks, and personnel buses roared past us, with sometimes a honk of the horn to indicate that the Stars and Stripes on Jim's knapsack had been observed.

Dropping down into Bar-le-Duc, with its sea of tile roofs, was ample compensation for having had to leave the towpath. It was like coming into the city in which the old king has just set the terms of competition for the hand of his beautiful daughter Princess Fairlinde. Except that the storybook city would not have had on its outskirts a grim monument commemorating the gunning down of twenty members of the F.F.I. (Forces Françaises de l'Intérieur) or Resistance.

Bar-le-Duc was full of U.S. Army personnel. After a month of talking with people whose knowledge of America was both slight and inaccurate, it was heady to chat with a Californian, two Vermonters, a fellow from Maine, a librarian from Minneapolis, and an Army wife from Colorado.

This well-intentioned Coloradan told us about a U.S. snack bar where we could get real hamburgers and milkshakes. We feigned indifference. As great internationalists, as world travelers bent on new experiences, we had not come to France to eat hamburgers!

World War II was all around us. A day later at Ligny, a citizen of that town was to explain why André Barrois's statue no longer stood in the square. During the war, it had been melted down for cannons.

We'd be finding other pedestals empty for the same reason. David would pick up a bullet-holed German helmet in the brush at the roadside. Signs still pointed the way to air-raid shelters. Monuments listed civilians deported by the Germans, never to return.

These days in Lorraine brought the war unhappily close. Nor could we feel too comfortable about the fact that the U.S. Army was now garrisoning Europe. Signs saying Americans Go Home didn't offend us, for we knew to whom they were addressed.

More immediate and decidedly hostile was an encounter near a canal lock in Lorraine. The warning *"chien méchant"* had been everywhere, but only here, on the thirty-second day of our trip, did a bad dog actually threaten us. He was lying quietly inside his *niche* beside the towpath when we walked past heedlessly. Like the dog that guarded the fabled tinderbox, he leapt out snarling, and Jim had his long-awaited opportunity to use his rake-handle walking stick as a weapon. That dog of Lorraine surely thought twice before ever again acting mean toward pedestrians speaking a strange language.

Another thing that struck us as we got deeper into Lorraine was the increasingly German character of the architecture, the faces, and eventually the tongue. Though everything we'd read indicated that the Lorrainers, like the Alsatians, had been glad to pass back from German governance to French, we wondered if they had not suffered some schizophrenia in the matter, so Germanic did this region seem.

On and off, when it suited us, we followed the towpaths. Since the country was becoming more mountainous, the locks were closer together. The Vosges Mountains rose steep to the east.

Wooden shoes became commoner. Strings of onions hung drying beside doorways. Women knelt at public washing places along the canal and at streamsides. Crocheted curtains at windows awakened memories of my Lorrainer grandmother and great-aunt, who had crotcheted everything—bedspreads, curtains, doilies, tablecloths, antimacassars.

Window boxes bloomed brightly. Dung spattered the village streets. (A Frenchman from another province told us that the reason window boxes bloom so brightly in Lorraine is precisely because the streets are full of dung.)

Near Commercy a great flock of blackbirds rose in a noisy cloud from a yellow grain field, for all the world like a reenactment of a Van Gogh painting. We had seen Cézanne's card players in cafes, and Manet's boaters on the rivers. Walking in France made us love the French painters more, as they had in the first place prepared us to love France.

At Commercy, during a before-dinner walk to inspect the magnificent Place du Fer de Cheval (Horseshoe Square) a newspaper reporter interviewed us. Throughout the conversation we were mindful of our role as unofficial goodwill ambassadors. We raved about the scenery, the people, and the food and were very modest about our feat of walking and our knowledge of the language. The children, who knew us well, weren't taken in by our humility. They were just too eager to get to dinner to waste words on it.

Over after-dinner cherry liqueurs came one of the strange multi-lingual conversations that cropped up every so often during our travels in France.

At a nearby table were two Dutch couples. Like many Dutch, they knew a great deal of English, and we could simply have chatted with them in our native tongue. But after the newspaper interview, pride had us in her toils. Jim insisted on speaking French. They knew a very little. I chose German, dredging up imperfect bits from beneath twenty years' moss. They spoke it correctly, but with obvious distaste. To cap my pride, I threw in gratis a touch of Dutch, which I fancied I knew something about from having compared a few German words with their Dutch equivalents. For an hour or so, these well-bred, kindly people put up with our effrontery, coming to our rescue with perfect English only when they saw we were really stuck.

Art, education, politics, food, drink, travel, plumbing—we talked about everything. At the end, the eight of us (or rather the six, for the children kept quite mum) were conversing alone in the dining room as the waiters finally extinguished the lights.

Drunk with delight at our glamorous "polyglotism," Jim and I said *bonne nuit* and led our little cavalcade upstairs where David and Eve waited until the bedroom door was closed.

"Why didn't you just talk English?" they said.

"Go to bed," we chorused.

TROUSSEY, UNIQUE TROUSSEY

MY forty-sixth birthday commenced with a beautiful box of my favorite marzipan that had been carried deep in Jim's knapsack from Bar-le-Duc. I didn't hesitate to eat some for breakfast.

It rained on and off that day. We'd had rain before, goodness knows, but there was a distinctiveness to the rain of Lorraine. From the manure piles in village streets during a rain trickled countless freshets of yellow slime. Between showers the manure piles gave off clouds of sickening vapor. It was chemistry vs. us.

Toward midafternoon—cold, wet, and hungry—we came upon Troussey. At first we couldn't tell. Was it a village? Yes, sure enough, there it was behind piles of *fumier*. How could so small a place have so many animals associated with it? Perhaps there was something we didn't know. Had some lucky farmer been digging a well and struck dung? Or was it a contest, like the outdoor Christmas lighting contests at home?

Just visible over the top of one pile we spied our good-luck sign, *la carotte,* and began picking our way closer. On the house was a IV° (fourth grade) cafe license as well. It was either continue eight kilometers or make do with Troussey. It was no time to be "choussey."

Like scores of cafes we'd been in, this one was furnished with plain wooden tables and benches, lighted by too few and too small windows. The walls were bare except for two or three advertisements and archaic calendars, plus the omnipresent Law Against Drunkenness.

There being no other customers at the time, we draped our raincoats over one table and seated ourselves at a second. Out of the back room came Madame, old and pretty. We liked her at once.

Our hearts were set on tea to warm us up. "Je regrette. Je n'ai pas de thé." She had no tea. We were crushed.

But David, unpredictable character, took from his knapsack a small, nasty-looking object, stating that it was a used tea bag from shipboard. It seemed he'd brought it along "for survival." (He also had book matches, a compass, and pins for making fishhooks.)

Could Madame perhaps let us have some boiling water, we asked. We would naturally pay.

"Mais oui." ("Of course.")

I was bringing out left-over breakfast croissants and sausage. Would we care to warm our food in her kitchen? I declined her sweet offer, but something prompted me to accept the woman-to-woman invitation to see her kitchen.

There was no range in it, but a huge deep fireplace at which she did all her cooking. On the hearth was a small earthenware casserole. A kettle hung from a hook over the coals, which she immediately stirred up.

Monsieur sat near by, smoking and regarding me with faint wonder.

An alcove a few feet from the fireplace contained their big double bed, up one step from the bare floor and framed by blue and white curtains. Along with the matching coverlet, the curtains gave to the otherwise cheerless room a look of human love and warmth.

The old lady took a teapot from the cupboard and filled it from the kettle. It was well water, she told me. There was not even a pump in the kitchen, let alone a faucet. Upon my own suggestion, I carried the teapot into the other room. She followed with cups and saucers and then retired.

Both Jim and I were suspicious of the great speed with which this alleged *eau bouillante* had been produced. It was no more boiling than the Danube is blue. He stuck his finger in it to prove it.

"Now's the time to use our chlorazene," I suggested. Tap water in any French hamlet was not to be trusted—least of all well water in a village that probably held the world manure title. So into the pot along with the old tea bag went a couple of chlorazene tablets from the first aid kit to kill the germs. Then a third one for luck. Eve added a sugar cube she'd been saving to give some fortunate horse or donkey. We stirred it all around and poured out a bit for Jim to taste.

With a look of supreme sacrifice, he announced he would add some of the rum he carried for "medicinal use." This further reduced the temperature of the murky mess, without at all disguising the chlorine taste. Unanimously we decided, wet and chilled though we were, that the cold water in our canteens (bottled spring water bought that morning at Commercy) was preferable.

Dave carried the pot to the door and poured out its contents onto the cobblestones, where it joined the saffron trickles from a nearby manure pile. It will be a long time before the gutters of Troussey again run with precisely that mixture.

DADDY GLEANS A NUGGET

THESE days in Lorraine offered a problem or two. There was the time we thought we had it made, with a peaceful canal day ahead of us; then the ordinarily smooth dirt of the towpath changed to coarse sharp gravel. Even to our toughened feet, even with the inner soles we'd added, it was murderous. All right, so we took to the highway. We were soon presented with a grand stretch of freshly tarred surface. Unless we jumped aside ever so nimbly, passing cars splattered us with black blobs.

There was the time we were unexpectedly excluded from the towpath. Pedestrians were barred from that section because of factory sites along the canal. Back to the highway!

Beyond the factories the highway crossed *under* the canal. Hopefully we climbed the embankment, thinking that now we could surely get back to the peace of the towpath. So we could. But I noted on the map that a few miles farther on, this canal of ours, the Meuse Canal, was going to cross another, the Marne-au-Rhin Canal. I had no idea how this intersection would take place. In my mind's eye I could see us arriving at the crossing, and no way for us to traverse the Marne-au-Rhin to continue on the Meuse. Eve would likely favor hailing a bargeman and asking him to take us across. Or would she suggest swimming the fifty feet, having first tossed the knapsacks over? Dave would offer to throw a line to a tree on the far side so we could go over Tarzan style. Or he'd propose making a reed raft. Jim would simply give me a dirty look and command an about-face.

That's the trouble with being in charge of maps and route planning. When everything goes right, no one notices. When something goes wrong, the air is blue with unuttered curses.

I bravely acknowledged my qualms and so we stayed with the highway. I'd give a lot to know how it would have worked out.

When we realized that Poste-de-Veleine, the place the Colorado Army wife had mentioned, was on our itinerary for the day, we decided with one accord to eat a light breakfast and save our appetites for hamburgers and milkshakes. During the morning when we stopped at the roadside to rest, we took only water.

Around noon—our heads filled with thoughts of chocolate, vanilla, and strawberry ("maybe even pineapple or raspberry"), thoughts of "well done with everything on"—we reached Poste-de-Veleine. The sentry at the gate grinned understandingly when we explained our quest. He looked approvingly at our U.S. passport. But alas, he informed us that the only money that would buy hamburgers and shakes at the snack bar was U.S. Army scrip. Not French money.

"Well, that's all right," said Jim. "We have American Express travelers checks."

Not even those.

Wishing we had never met that Army wife in Bar-le-Duc, we trudged on about fifty feet and sat on a bank within sight of the post gate. Once more it was bread and sausage for us, and canned milk mixed with water.

Full but frustrated, we were putting away the plastic glasses and getting ready to start on when the noncom in charge of sentries emerged from Poste-de-Veleine.

"Hello, folks," he said. "I heard you were wanting to come in and eat at the snack bar. I'd sure be pleased to treat you."

With profuse thanks, we declined. Wherever that young man is, I wish him happiness. If he's still in the Army, may he receive from compatriot, ally, and enemy alike, the kind of warm and human treatment he extended to us.

The weather continued rainy. We were forever stopping to put on or take off our raincoats. Even the natives were losing their patience with *la pluie.*

With the rain there came out of hiding some of the biggest, ugliest, slimiest, yellow slugs imaginable. These harmless, repulsive creatures so unnerved Eve that she would sometimes lie awake at night, silently weeping at the mere thought of them. She and I always shared a room, often a bed. It was thanks to those mustard-colored slugs that, to distract her into sleep, I related to her, serial fashion, the life of Albert Schweitzer.

But Lorraine had its good points too. It was there that we met a shepherd tending his flock. He wore a long, full, black coat that must sometimes have been a pretty good substitute for a tent. One end of his staff was a crook of the conventional kind, for hooking round a sheep's neck. The other had a sharp metal point which, he told us, was for prying stones out of sheep's hooves.

We had no stones in our hooves, but we did have to seek expert care for our shoes. Of course Lorraine wasn't the first place where we sought a *cordonnerie*. On and off for 360 miles we'd been going into little shops and cajoling cobblers into making this or that repair *sur le champ* ("at once"). The idea of while-you-wait shoe service had yet to invade France; but with a canny blend of pathos and flattery, Jim always managed to win out. Indeed, we had to have our quick repairs, for we'd brought no other shoes. Occasionally we would even track *monsieur le cordonnier* to his home and persuade him to return to his shop.

Without exception we found these artisans able and obliging. Sometimes they'd talk freely with us, as the cobbler at Châlons had done. Before he had installed five pairs of the metal plates that we all wore front and back, he'd given us his entire financial situation. He wasn't complaining, but it certainly was a gloomy picture. His wife worked. They lived with her father who also worked. They raised most of their vegetables in their *potager*. Even so, after taxes and necessities were paid, he and his wife could afford only a week's vacation, with one liter of *essence* ("gasoline") for their *moto* ("motorbike") and a *tente* to sleep in. It made us feel ashamed of our good fortune.

What little they had these Lorrainers seemed willing to share. An old woman came hobbling out of her house on her cane, exchanged a few words with us, and offered us a drink of water. Her heart was obviously pure. We weren't so sure of her *eau,* and, as gracefully as possible, we declined it.

She showed us her son's picture, in uniform.

"Ah," said Jim, observing the stripes on the youth's sleeve, "a lieutenant!"

"Non," she replied. The photographer had put those on to make a better picture. Well, we'd be the last to begrudge the young man his instant promotion.

It was in Lorraine that we met two Parisians, Monsieur Kanter and his son. The father was a cabinetmaker of Russian extraction and evidently made better wages than our cobbler friend. He and his son were on an extensive bicycle tour of northern France. Later, to my amazement, I was to encounter M. Kanter on the streets of

Strasbourg, a city of two hundred thousand inhabitants. To be in a foreign place, convinced you are utterly without friends or acquaintances, and then run into someone you know—it's wonderful.

Making good on our promise to Eve that she would see the birthplace of Jeanne d'Arc, we took a day out at Nancy, hired a car and driver, and drove to Domrémy and back. How amazing to learn that in Jeanne's day, Domrémy was not in France but in the Duchy of Lorraine! Thus another prime figure in French history turns out not to have been born in France proper.

It was at Domrémy that we heard of a feat of walking beside which our own surely paled. Catholics receive indulgences for making the pilgrimage to the birthplace of Jeanne. If they make it on foot they receive extra indulgences. For still more indulgences, one man had made it (distance unknown) with dried peas in his shoes.

Even with nearly four hundred miles behind us, even with some of the finest calluses of the twentieth century, we knew that this man was made of sterner stuff than we. Split peas, flat side up, would have done us in—let alone round dried peas!

Eve had had her "artichokhea." I had had my yellow leg, Dave his toe. Jim alone seemed proof against all shafts. But as inexorably as the plot of a Greek tragedy unfolds, his turn was coming. He had an aversion to donning his raincoat and would often insist that we others put on ours while he granted himself a sort of royal immunity. Between Lunéville and Blamont, he started coming down with one of his bad chest colds.

"How far is it to Blamont, Binkie?"

"Fifteen kilometers."

"Is it a sizable place?"

"Not very," I apologized. "On the map it looks about the size of Gournay." Gournay of infamous memory. Why did I have to select that for comparison?

He groaned. "Well, what do you know about our hotel?"

"Nothing, except that it's named Hôtel de Commerce, and that we have a reservation there."

There followed a few moments of silence. We had stayed before in places called Hôtel de Commerce.

"Well," he wished aloud, "maybe it's better than it sounds. If I could just have a good hot bath and spend the night in a good bed in a warm, dry room, I could beat this thing."

We walked along in silence, pausing now and then for him to cough, hawk, and spit, and—I must add—to curse. "About the size of Gournay, eh?"

Finally we sighted Blamont, dropping down into it, as we had into many a night's stop. On the very edge of town stood a fine large building of modern construction, with many windows.

"That's it," Jim exulted. "There's our Hôtel de Commerce. They're bound to have private baths, lots of hot water, everything I need."

Another hundred paces and we descried the familiar blue white and red shield and the word *Gendarmerie*. Alas, it was the district barracks for state police. Even if we could have insinuated ourselves into their fine modern building, we knew it contained no such comfort and privacy as we were dreaming of.

The Hôtel de Commerce, when we found it, was modest indeed. Up a narrow winding stairway we were led to two connecting rooms, neither of which had running water, hot or cold. There were bowls and pitchers and chamber pots. The building was cold and damp. No need to feel the bed linen to know that it too was cold and damp.

The farther of the two rooms—more like an overgrown closet—contained Eve's and my bed, a small cast-iron stove, and a vast supply of wood. No kindling, no paper. It was madness even to think we could use the stove. The wood was simply stored there to keep it comparatively dry. Who ever heard of a French hotelkeeper providing heat before October first?

Tired and hungry, we dumped our knapsacks on the beds, used bowl and pitcher, and went downstairs.

Ten-year-old Eve was the only member of the family who could pass erect through the door that led to the dining room. As we sat waiting for our *potage*, we studied this Alice in Wonderland portal and decided it might originally have been a fireplace. If only it would grow no smaller during dinner, and we no larger, all would be well.

Dinner was not the best. It included no part of the huge tub of mushrooms the grandfather was preparing at a nearby table. But it was food, and it raised our spirits—even Jim's.

Yet there was the night upstairs to be faced. True, he had started a course of antibiotics which we'd brought along for just such an occasion. True, Madame, upon questioning, produced some extra-strong licorice cough drops. But as we filed out, plucky little band crouching through tiny door, we knew a rough time awaited us.

Togetherness, watchword of our walking trips and of our family philosophy, was too much of a good thing that long, cramped night at Blamont. The two little rooms resounded intermittently with all the loathsome noises of a juicy bronchitis. Little sleep was had.

At one point, Dave, whose lot it was to share a room with his father, sat up in bed as Jim paced the floor. "Can I go in Mama and Eve's room? You're keeping me awake."

Jim turned on him. "Your father is very sick. He may die. Go back to sleep." Dave lay down again. What had made him think there was room for another in our closet anyway? Or that sleep was possible there?

I was seriously concerned about Jim, and in the small hours when both children finally were asleep, he and I whispered gravely together. We both wanted very much to finish what we had undertaken, the cross-country walk. But no feat of that kind was worth risking a dangerous illness. We decided that if his condition did not take a definite turn for the better by morning, we would hire a car and get to Strasbourg and a first-rate doctor as fast as we could. Certainly nothing was to be gained by staying in this damp, cold Hôtel de Commerce.

Somehow the night passed. In the morning Jim was better. Whether it was antibiotics, extra-strong licorice, or sheer will to finish the trip on foot, he was better.

When Madame brought our breakfast tray as arranged the previous evening, she was all solicitude. And how had *monsieur* slept? Had the cough drops aided? What *espèce* of night had he passed?

Not one to mince words, Jim replied that he had had a terrible night, that he had slept *pas du tout*, not at all, that it had been the worst *nuit* of his life.

"Ah! Une nuit blanche!" ("A white night.") She set the tray down and left in a murmur of commiseration.

Jim repeated her words. "Une nuit blanche. Did you get that, Binkie? Une nuit blanche. That's an idiom to remember." And we knew he would survive.

FINISH WITH A FLOURISH

IT was Alsace now, the last province of our eastward trek. The forested slopes of the Vosges Mountains stretched away on every hand. Fields of tobacco, fields of hops. Our shoes, wet for several days, began to dry out under the Alsatian sun. The word *Strasbourg* began to appear on milestones. The architecture had a German flavor. People were bilingual.

As we entered one place and asked directions, the man replied, "Ersten Strasse links, et tout droit." He wasn't even aware he'd shifted midsentence from German to French.

I had unlimbered my German a bit with those courteous Dutch people at Commercy, but now in Alsace I really began to swing. The family was impressed. Although Jim had long ago heard all about my five months in Munich back in the thirties and my bike tours in the Bavarian Alps, he'd never witnessed any real proof that I had a useful knowledge of German. He was glad to have me along.

A charming blonde who looked like Marguerite in *Faust* paused in her haying to chat with us in French. The young people of Alsace and Lorraine speak French, and the older ones German, she said. But all generations understand both, she assured us.

From time to time when it was practical, we walked the canal towpath. Locks were still more frequent, for we were climbing, climbing.

Wistful thoughts of hamburgers and milkshakes stirred again as signs appeared announcing, between Sarrebourg and Saverne, a U.S. Air Force base. Again we were rebuffed.

Perhaps it was sour grapes, but the more we thought about it, the more we felt that Army or Air Force hamburgers and shakes would have been ill at ease anyway, inside of people so disapproving of Uncle Sam as world policeman.

Hamburgerless, we plodded to the thirteen-hundred-foot summit of Saut-de-St-Charles (St. Charles Jump-off) and took a plunging wooded trail down to Saverne, where true Alsatian fare awaited us: *choucroute garnie* ("sauerkraut with everything").

Saverne, like a Bruges of Alsace, had canal views of prime picturesque quality, complete with washboard stones at people's back doors. The only member of the family with a real taste for sauerkraut, I fell head over heels in love with three rows of cabbage—red, purple, and white.

"Why would anyone want a picture of cabbages?" demanded Jim as I pushed the shutter button.

"Why did you want her to take that picture of empty wine bottles?" asked David.

Beyond Saverne the wooded green waves of the Vosges lay dark and Germanic under overcast skies, but rain it did not. Our six-week walk, begun and pursued under such adverse weather conditions, was coming to a reasonably dry end.

In the fields it was tobacco, anise, grapevines; it was hops growing tall on wires. In the cafes it was the hearty smells of beer, *schnitzel*, *roggenbrot*. Gone was the hard-crusted, slightly sour, white-centered French bread of which we'd consumed such quantities. We missed it but fell to and liked the rye bread.

Next to occasional inescapable use of a heavily traveled highway, the hardest thing about a walking trip is the stretch entering a big city. There's traffic. There's confusion about street names and the location of the hotel. Sometimes there's even congestion on the sidewalks.

Accordingly, an early start was in order for August 12. Strasbourg lay at day's end. We were exhilarated to think that our grand and simple design of walking across France was near completion. With a sense of history being made, we said goodby to our last *gîte,* saying it, in effect, to all the twenty-eight other night shelters we'd left behind.

Some had been grubby, some deluxe, some ancient, some *très moderne,* some cramped, some commodious. But one and all they had shared three constants: thin walls, bolsters, and clammy sheets.

The thin walls had seldom bothered us; even though every word of our neighbors' talk might be audible, we were usually so wholesomely tired that we were asleep almost the moment we hit the pillow (or bolster). The bolsters we'd learned to use, if by chance there were no pillows.

The clammy sheets we excused because of the unseasonably wet year. We weren't the first walkers to encounter damp sheets. Coleridge complained of the same thing on an English walking trip. Said the maid to him: The sheets couldn't possibly be damp, because they'd been slept in already two or three times that week! To the everlasting honor of La Belle France, be it said we never doubted we were the first to sleep between those damp sheets.

So, with the usual check to see that every last item was in someone's knapsack, we left Wasselonne early. It was Sunday. The town was still asleep. Along its streets, its narrow alleys and stairways, the shutters were closed. It was a fine sunny morning, a perfect day for winding up a great trip.

Though some of the four might have denied it, there was more than a touch of sadness, now that it was almost over.

The Kronthal (Crown Valley) was verdant. Our route lay through a succession of hamlets—Nordheim, Küttolsheim, Quatzenheim, Hürtigheim, Stützheim. Always the red tile roofs and the tall church spire of some *heim* visible somewhere near or far.

Church bells were ringing. Villagers dressed in their sober black best gathered in front of a church here, issued out of a church there. Young people, scrubbed and combed and in their best, rode past us on bikes, returning our greeting but seldom initiating an exchange.

Finally there came into view, miles away, the single spire of Strasbourg's lopsided, never-finished cathedral. Seated under a tree where we could appreciate the sight, we had a snack of rye bread and canned paté, with the now-ritual diluted canned milk.

"Mama, something seems to have happened here," said Dave. It surely had. The entire side seam of one trouser leg had ripped, baring his fine sturdy calf. Out came the sewing kit, off came the slacks, and in no time he was proper and decent for the entry into Strasbourg.

To make it more festive, Jim tied wildflowers to the upper end of his walking stick.

As we neared the city, following a disused interurban right-of-way, the cathedral tower grew bigger and bigger. Suddenly then, we were there.

We had walked 750 kilometers, 470 miles, from Le Havre on the English Channel to Strasbourg on the River Rhine. We would, the following day, walk through the city to the river itself and cross into Germany for good measure. But to all intents the mission had been accomplished.

Not once had we accepted a ride. Indeed, only once had we been offered one. This was not surprising since in France it's against the law to *faire des pouces* ("make thumbs"), and surely likewise illegal to pick up those who make thumbs.

Our daily average worked out to something better than fifteen miles per walking day. There was still enough antiseptic mouthwash to get us to an American drug store.

Dinner was a festive, silly meal that must have caused some mystification among any waiters who eavesdropped.

"Aujourd'hui, Madame," Jim said to me, recalling my prize boner in French. In some little village early in the trip I'd had a particularly long and exhausting French conversation in a shop. I had dug up words I didn't know I knew, and had made lucky stabs at others. Leaving the shop in a state of mental exhaustion, I meant to bid the woman goodby ("Au revoir, Madame") but instead enunciated with great clarity and aplomb "Aujourd'hui, Madame" ("To-day, Madam").

In reprisal, I taunted Jim with a blooper of his. At Lunéville, his eagerness to render courtesy and respect to a Catholic priest had so rattled him that at 9 A.M. he'd greeted the priest with "Bon soir, Père" ("Good evening, Father").

Eve reminded us of the time Jim had said *fromage* when he meant *potage,* telling an amazed waitress that we would begin our meal with cheese (instead of soup). Epicurean heresy of the worst kind!

"Well, it all depends on which *tabatière* you get your information from, doesn't it, Dave?" quipped Jim, and the kids erupted in laughter at this reference to a daring guess of mine. In an after-dinner discussion with French people at some hotel, I had meant to say that I'd received such-and-such information from the tobacco-shop lady. *"De la tabatière,"* I said. For a split second my listeners had registered surprise, which was immediately replaced by *politesse.* *Tabac* is tobacco. How was I to know that a *tabatière* is not a lady tobacconist but a snuffbox?

Our timing had been excellent. The next day, August 13, was our wedding anniversary, and after walking through the city and across the bridge to set foot on German soil, we came back to Strasbourg and dined in style to celebrate nineteen years of "lucky in love."

We were celebrating more than that. Perhaps we were puffed up, but Jim and I felt like a couple of jungle explorers who've brought their safari to a successful conclusion. On my shoulders had rested the responsibility of mapping, planning, working out the details. On his, as head of the family and decision maker, had lain the general responsibility for our health, safety, and solvency. We had proved to ourselves that we could conceive and execute, even with the children, a project of fairly heroic proportions.

After a couple of anniversary cocktails, we were expansively discussing the locale of our next walking trip, working out on paper how long it would take to save the necessary money and making drawings of the kind of knapsacks we wanted. Came the wine, and we envisioned a boundless career of walking trips. This just couldn't be the end. The sky was the limit! We'd walk all over the earth!

While the two of us carried on our rhapsodic dialogue oblivious of the children, they had been having their own conversation. Apparently it had had to do with some permission withheld by us the previous winter for some youthful adventure and with our alleged reasons for withholding said permission. When we surfaced to listen, ten-year-old Eve was saying to thirteen-year-old Dave, in obvious reference to us, "That's all very well for them. They've had their lives." Had our lives?

PART III
New England to New France

OFF ON A ZIGZAG

IF we were to have another all-family walking trip, it would have to be soon. David was now sixteen and quite convinced that "family stuff" was for the birds. Naturally, he was using every wile to bring Eve under his corrupt influence.

Wistfully we thought of walking again in Europe, but getting there would be costly. Besides, the sky over Europe was darkening. We had visions of being stranded at the outbreak of war. Best to stay on our own continent. We could always walk home. But where on our continent?

"We could walk to Nicaragua and see Uncle Arthur and Auntie Helen," suggested Eve.

"We could walk the Appalachian Trail," said Dave, momentarily forgetting that he took no interest in "family stuff."

"We could walk the Erie Canal, and some of those other old canals," I offered vaguely. "It would be like France."

"French Canada is obviously the place to go," announced Jim. He was still teaching French both privately and in the night school and was more than ever in love with that language. "Quebec is more than 80 percent French speaking. We'll talk French every step of the way. We only scratched the surface when we went to Gaspé." It was settled. Groans from the young.

Newport, Vermont, at the southern tip of twenty-three-mile-long Lake Memphrémagog, was shrouded in dispiriting fog when we arrived by train at evening on July 24. In an unheated lakeside cabin among the pines, we spent an inauspicious first night.

I huddled in my sweater and pored over the map once more—with a sinking feeling that our projected walk from Newport northeast to Quebec City and thence southwest to Montreal would be anticlimactic after the trip across France.

Would it lack newness, be only a sort of poor man's France? Would it be French enough to satisfy Jim? After all, it was part of the British Commonwealth. Would the rebel forces, led by David, prove too much for us?

In any event, we were all four prepared to make the trip count for something. I had brought in my knapsack the first half of a two-year textbook on music theory, for I had resolved to enroll in a second-year class at Coe College when we returned. If I were going to test out of first year, I'd need to snatch study time here and there on the trip.

Jim, armed with pocket dictionary and a head fuller than ever of French grammar and vocabulary, was eager to speak as much French as possible and to hear more of the curious accent and provincial usages of which we'd had a taste in Gaspé.

Eve had her oboe reed. The instrument itself would have been too bulky and too heavy to carry, but by practicing on the reed, she could keep her "lip."

Dave, who we suspected would keep his own kind of lip regardless, had brought along Morse code to learn.

The somewhat zigzag course I'd plotted through the *Cantons de l'Est* ("Eastern Townships") would, we hoped, get us to the city of Quebec in time to celebrate our twenty-second anniversary. After that we'd see about time and money to go on to Montreal.

The morning sky boded another rainy walking trip. Amid grumbling, ponchos and plastic raincoats were extracted from knapsacks and the remaining contents rearranged.

We set out in the drizzle. Jim, shapelessly draped in his Army surplus poncho, headed the column as usual. David, likewise in poncho, was already chafing at having to "always walk behind Daddy." Eve, in plastic raincoat and rainhat, had been emancipated from the red rubbers but didn't evince commensurate joy about that. I, likewise in plastic coat and hat, was as glum as the others, having reluctantly decided I must stow my camera in my knapsack. A great way to start my first attempt at color sliding a walking trip!

To make sure we were getting off on the right road, I stole a last-minute look at the map. On it, I saw for the first time, over on the far shore of Lake Memphrémagog, a tiny cross.

ANOTHER WORLD, ANOTHER TIME

BY the time we reached the Dominion frontier at Beebe Plain, we'd have been glad to have the drizzle back. We were afoot in Quebec at the outset of a heat wave that would damage crops, ruin dispositions, and make banner headlines all over the province. Not the wettest summer but the hottest. Chalk up one for Jim, who had insisted on our carrying seven one-quart canteens.

At Beebe we consumed the first of scores of Canadian milkshakes that would supplement the canteens and cool us on our way. The Canadian milkshake was a rather poor relation of the real American thing, but far, far better than no milkshake at all.

At first the population seemed to be about a fifty-fifty mixture: approximately half the names on farm mailboxes were English and about half were French—including, as first names, Charlemagne and Napoleon.

Jim would size up an approaching pedestrian or cyclist, or someone working in a field, and offer a greeting, *"Bonjour"* or "Good morning," according to his judgment. Just often enough to add spice to the children's day, he got a reply in the opposite language.

It was impossible to size up a dog. But to get rid of a bothersome one, if "Go home!" didn't work, *"Va t'en!"* did.

Seldom was it the natives who spoke first. They observed us with guarded curiosity. There was no question here, as there had been in France, of our being mistaken for people of some hated nationality. They must have known we were Americans, but, *mon Dieu,* even the screwball Yankee had never before turned up in Quebec Province walking along the back roads in a family foursome, wearing knapsacks!

People in the fields to whom we waved usually replied with a mute stare. Children, seeing us approach, would run into the farmhouse and peek out from behind lace curtains. One little girl was in such panic that, running from us, she lost a shoe but went on without it.

At first there was confusion about place names. The name on my map didn't always correspond with the official village-limit sign as we entered a community. For example, "Katevale" on the map turned out to be "Ste-Catherine" according to the sign. Evidently provincial mapmakers were less French, less religious-minded, than local authorities. I'd have to keep my wits about me, to see that we stayed on course.

Long, skinny Lake Memphrémagog (Indian for "beautiful water") from whose Vermont tip we'd set out and whose northern portion projects some twenty miles into Canada, has a shady, colorful history. It was a freeway for Prohibition Era rumrunners. By now its eastern shore was a popular resort and summer cabin region.

Fitch Bay, an arm of Memphrémagog on this eastern shore, was a fishing center where we hoped to roost after our first day's hike. The resort, booked full with anglers from both sides of the border, referred us to a charming family whose farm home stood beside a covered bridge that crossed Fitch Bay Narrows.

This old-fashioned bridge was by far the prettiest of the many we crossed on this trip.

"Tomorrow I'm going to wear three pairs of socks," Jim announced as we settled ourselves in the two pleasant, spotless rooms our hosts had shown us to. "If two pairs are a better cushion than one, three should be better than two."

He was still carrying, this trip, the walking stick he'd fashioned from a rake handle. The 573 miles it had done in Gaspé and France had given it a fine seasoned look. Moreover, it seemed to have gained distinction since we'd learned that Coleridge had made his stick from a broom handle.

Dinner up at the fishing resort restored us. Our overnight hosts loaned us the family rowboat for a twilight trip up the narrows. Fish were jumping, waterbirds were skimming in and out among the cattails, and something that looked like an otter slid into the water.

A discreet inquiry had revealed to me that the cross on the far shore of Memphrémagog represented a monastery. A plan had begun to hatch in my mind. Sure enough, the next day in the far distance across the lake there appeared a group of buildings that had to be some kind of institution.

"It's a monastery," I announced. "We've never been to a monastery. Why not go around there tomorrow from Magog?"

Jim could think of several reasons why not. It was hot enough on this side of the lake; over there hardly a tree was visible. Furthermore, it would take at least a day, probably two, and would throw us off schedule. Besides, we didn't even know they'd permit visitors.

The fields were already ripening toward August. Houses on farms and in villages had a flyaway nautical look, with their wide porches and wrought-iron outside stairways. Houses that weren't white were painted in cheerful, imaginative colors. In the yards, borders were marked with rows of burnt-out light bulbs that had been painted bright colors and stuck into the ground. Eve spotted the first wild huckleberries, and she and I lagged behind for a juicy, gluttonous few minutes.

David complained about having to wear a hat, and Jim informed him that without it he would suffer sunstroke.

It was 98 degrees in the shade. The sky was cloudless, a delft blue oven overhead. As we neared Magog at the northern tip of the lake, people were listlessly fanning themselves in swings on the lawns of lakeside villas.

Jim was finding three pairs of socks both softer and hotter. Eve too had become footsore after a sixteen-mile hike on only the second day out. In pidgin French she complained, "Donnez-moi ma feet back" ("Give me back my feet").

In the room she and I shared at the once-plush hotel in Magog, the bathtub was in a closet. The clothes hooks had been left, so it was a cinch to string up my clothesline for a good wash to drip over the tub. Magog's tub-in-a-closet was only the first of a number of bizarre bath arrangements we would encounter in Quebec.

With wife and two children against him, Jim soon gave in on the monastery and tried to phone St-Benoît-du-Lac to inquire whether the brothers could put us up the following night. Because of some indisposition of equipment or personnel, he couldn't get through to them, but we decided to risk it.

"Better get there before five," the hotel clerk advised. "That's when they have vespers."

There was no likelihood of milkshakes on the western shore between the head of the lake and the monastery. Fortunately, it was dirt road, a bit cooler to the feet than the asphalt of the day before. But there was little shade. It was ideal weather for pitching hay, which was just what farmers along the way were doing.

As fast as water was poured down our parched throats, it seemed to issue, salted, from our pores. "I told you seven canteens wouldn't be too many," Jim crowed.

The monastery towers would come into view and then disappear behind a hill, later to reappear—closer, more medieval, more imposing yet. One tower looked very odd.

At the junction where the road turned off for the monastery, there was a small crossroads store. The thermometer, in the shade, read 27 degrees Centigrade, which we hastily converted into 105 degrees Fahrenheit. It was four o'clock. Our canteen water was all but gone. After gulping down four bottles of ice-cold pop, we took off over the last range of hills. Now and then beyond the towers, there was a glimpse of the lake, shimmering silver in the heat.

Seriously concerned lest we arrive late and be turned away, Jim "poured it on" and the rest of us loped along behind him, breathless and sweating.

The Nun's Story, both as book and as film, had made a profound impression on Eve. Of the four of us, she was no doubt most excited by the prospect of a visit to St-Benoît-du-Lac. Even so, when we descended the last pitch toward the main buildings, passing an apple orchard and what looked like a long frame farmhouse, all of us were properly hushed.

The gap would be considerable between, on the one hand, four hot, dirty Americans who believed enthusiastically in the life of the here and now, and, on the other, members of an order that concerned itself with the life of the elsewhere and hereafter. We knew, of course, that it was up to us as monastery guests to try to make the giant leap and comprehend their point of view.

The curious effect created by the tallest tower, which we'd seen from some distance, had been the result of a scaffold around it. It was still being built. The monks themselves were doing the work—mixing mortar, carrying hods, climbing ladders—all in their black, ankle-length Benedictine robes and their open sandals. They were just finishing their day's labor. Poles apart, perhaps, in ways of looking at life, they and we were in at least one thing very close together: sweat.

One of them directed us, in French, to the host monk, *Dom* ("master") Pierre.

Jim and David were then taken to quarters in a kind of men's hostel; Eve and I were shown to the *maison des dames*, the ladies' guest house, which turned out to be the long white building in the apple orchard.

In it there were no double rooms. Though she was nearing her thirteenth birthday, Eve had never spent a night away from home in a room by herself. To have to do it first in a monastery seemed a bit scary, but she accepted it with only a small gulp. She and I had identical singles side by side.

Without taking the time to read the posted regulations, the two of us washed up and met our men to attend vespers in the solid stone chapel.

I knew that the Benedictine order has, since the early nineteenth century, made the purification, regeneration, and preservation of Gregorian chant one of its chief works. I was eager to hear this fountainhead of Western music in its authentic setting. But instead of a darkly gothic place, the chapel interior was bright, modern, and cheerful. Its light walls were decorated with geometric Indian motifs in strong, straightforward colors.

In the choir two double rows of stalls faced each other. Seated in them were some twenty black-robed monks. Other monks filled the front pews. Elsewhere, scattered here and there, were a few nuns—some in black, some in white—and a few lay visitors.

I could not get any medieval feeling. It was still the twentieth century. Then three more monks appeared at the altar and suddenly I was in the Middle Ages. From head to toe they were in pure white. The peaked hoods of their robes were drawn up over the heads so that almost nothing could be seen of their features. The face of Savonarola came to mind.

Since our departure from home, I'd been working daily on my music theory studies. Every morning I would wake earlier than the others, study my text, and work at exercises in my music tablet. Sometimes during the day when we'd take a roadside rest or cool-off, I'd use the time for writing four-part harmony—modulations, chord progressions, transpositions. Dave called it "making music, music, music."

Now, after all of that trying to hear chords, chords, chords, in my mind's ear, it was like a drink from a cool spring to listen to the chaste solo lines of melody coming a cappella from the faceless singers in white and the unison responses from the black-clad figures in the choir stalls.

After the first wave of medieval feeling had swept over me, I began to listen closely for modes: Dorian, Phrygian, Lydian. There was the magic of far places and vanished ages in those scales. The sounds woke stirrings in me, perhaps from some remote ancestor. *I couldn't very well be descended from a monk*, I thought irreverently as we came forth into the brilliant sunshine and the reality of scaffolds, ladders, and mortar-mixing troughs. And yet. . . .

Eve and I strolled back to the *maison des dames* with a lay organist who informed us we'd arrived at St-Benoît in the final hours of a special summer course in Gregorian chant. To attend the course, clergy and lay musicians had come not only from all over Canada but also from the United States. The St-Benoît choir, she told us, had won international honors.

Jim and Dave were to have supper with the men. The two of us were shown to the women's refectory in the basement of the *maison*. There, before sitting down at the single long table, we joined the nuns and the several female students of chant in prayer. The supper was simple; it was silent. The only words spoken were, in French or English: "Sister, would you like the bread?" a euphemism for "Please pass it."

For us, mealtime had always been the signal for narration of the day's events, for exchange of ideas, perhaps for argument and certainly for hilarity and joy. The silence was bizarre. To eat with other human beings and not talk!

It was soon over. Another prayer was said, and a burst of feminine chatter broke forth. The two nuns in tropical white told us they were at St-Benoît for rest and retreat between missionary assignments in Africa.

Eve and I saw our menfolk hardly at all that evening, but both contingents were storing up experiences and impressions to share later.

In the orchard it was beginning to be almost cool. Seated on a bench there, we chatted in French with a different organist, this one from Montreal. She and the other students of chant had had their last exams that day and would be leaving in the morning.

Now that the spell of the vesper service had somewhat worn off, I had had to admit to myself that, international honors notwithstanding, there'd been times when the monks had flatted. I asked her whether this happened often.

Without agreeing that they had flatted, she pointed out it would be understandable, since they were singing at the end of a full day's physical labor, some as construction workers on the new tower, others in the cheese factory, and so on. The singers, she pointed out, weren't a privileged class in monastery society, but did their part in all the activities of the place. There were the apple orchards to tend, apple syrup and cider to make and bottle, cows to tend, cheese to make.

I felt rather silly to have mentioned their faulty pitch. With the mercury at 105 degrees it was really a wonder they hadn't flatted more heinously.

Because of their heavy work schedule, the monks were relieved of the usual midnight vigils service. Instead, after complines was performed at seven in the evening, vigils followed at eight.

The four of us met for complines. To our uninitiate ears and minds, this service seemed pretty much like vespers—a blur of Latin, ceremonial gestures, and, again, the antiseptic lines of Gregorian chant.

Prière de ne pas fumer ("please do not smoke") said the small card posted in my room. As a nonsmoker, I could disregard both the request and the thoughtfully provided ashtray.

Posted also were hours of all the services: lauds at 5:20 A.M., mass at 6:30, prime at 7:15, communion at 7:45, tierce at 9, sext at 12, and so around to vespers at 5. As non-Catholics who had already attended vespers and complines, we felt we could safely be absent from the other six services.

Last item on the *horaire* or time schedule was: "9:30 P.M. *à* 5:20 A.M.—*grand silence.*" We were requested not to leave our rooms during that period and to refrain from making any unnecessary sound. As the mother of thirteen and sixteen year olds (children who since infancy had been prone to fill the upstairs, sometimes till nearly midnight, with illicit shouts and laughter) I liked that admonition.

If only there had been some way to institute *le grand silence* in a certain Iowa home!

AN AFTER-DINNER DIN

THE bells that summoned the faithful to lauds at 5:20 A.M. roused me to my study of music theory.

"That wasn't much of a breakfast," Eve remarked to David when the four of us met, knapsacks packed, ready to set out. "All we had was fruit and cold biscuits and cold cereal. What did you have?"

"Same. Daddy wouldn't let me drink the milk because it wasn't *pasteurisé.*"

"Same here."

"He wouldn't even let me put it on my cereal."

"Same here."

"Well," I remarked self-righteously, "it wasn't much for people like us, but at least we only have to walk. They have to build a tower on a breakfast like that."

"Who was it who wanted to visit a monastery anyway?" inquired the man at the head of the line.

Rarely on a walking trip did we retrace our steps, but there was no other route by which to regain Magog. Besides, we were too busy to be bored—busy being hot, busy comparing notes.

Eve and I, it seemed, had missed a ritual hand washing. In the men's refectory they'd been lined up according to protocol: first the monastery brothers, then the visiting clergy, then the visiting lay Catholics, then Jim and Dave, and lastly a troop of Boy Scouts. One by one, they stepped up to the father abbot, who ceremonially laved each pair of hands with water from a silver ewer. Another monk wiped them—all with one towel. "A dandy way to pass germs around," commented Jim.

As in the women's refectory, there'd been prayers before and after each *repas,* and those at the table had been silent throughout the meal. But over a public address system in the men's refectory had come continually the voice of one of the brothers at the monks' table, reading in French from a text on Gregorian chant—a text published by the monastery.

When Jim had asked what we owed for food and lodging, he'd been told there was no charge, but that a gift would not be refused. We were glad to contribute to the institution that had given us such a memorable experience and sorry not to be able to buy and carry away several bottles of luscious-looking St-Benoît apple syrup.

Thanks to our seven canteens, we didn't dry up and blow away on the way back to Magog. Thanks to a small, blessed creek beside which we had stopped the previous day en route to the monastery, we had one deliciously cool snack break.

At a crossroad a Scotsman hailed us and asked in heatherish accent what we were about. Learning of our plan to walk to Quebec and then Montreal he replied, "Well, my name is Walkerrrr, but I couldna do what you'rrrre doin'."

"I could do with a bit of your relative right now, Mr. Walker," said Jim. (I thought I detected a trace of Highlands in his voice.)

"Johnny Walkerrrr's no frrrriend o' mine," replied the exceptional Scot.

Some miles later, nearing Magog again, we sought much-needed liquid refreshment (though not whiskey); pop for the children, for us, ale. Canadian ale was reputed to be good, and it was time to find out if that was true.

There was some confusion about bottle sizes, and Jim and I

found ourselves each with what looked like a quart. Dehydrated though we were, we couldn't make it to the bottoms of those bottomless bottles.

People were talking of nothing but the heat wave. For the next day, Eve's birthday, we had a twenty-one-mile stint. It was 120 degrees in the sun, and it seemed to be all sun, except immediately under our hat brims.

"How can you stand three pairs of socks on your feet in weather like this?" Eve asked.

"Well," Jim replied, "I was just thinking I might wear four pairs tomorrow. If my feet get hot enough, maybe they'll forget how sore they are."

We drank the contents of our seven canteens and refilled some of them. And made seven stops for pop.

"I hate wearing this dumb hat," David grumped. "Only sissies wear hats."

Jim waxed eloquent. "You'd hate sunstroke even worse. Death by sunstroke is a horrible death."

"Dit-dit-dit-dit . . . dit . . . dit-dah-dit-dit . . . dit-dah-dit-dit!"

"What does that spell?" Eve whispered to Dave.

"I won't tell you, but it rhymes with 'spell.' "

"Mama! He swore in Morse code!"

Arrived at Sherbrooke, we were too exhausted to hunt immediately for our hotel. But the first cafe we encountered, a modest one, had not only the milkshakes two of us wanted instead of dinner, but, providentially, a tiny chocolate cake and thirteen candles for Eve's party.

Anyway they told us later at the hotel, the dining room there had closed down hours before "because of the heat."

For all its English-sounding name, Sherbrooke had four French-speaking inhabitants for every English speaker, and nine Catholics for every Protestant. It was a manufacturing center, a place of sixty-three thousand people. It was bustling and sophisticated, like a miniature New World Paris. Most impressive of all—it had a public library, the first we'd seen since the United States, the first of only three we were to see on our trek through scores of French-Canadian towns.

"Nobody reads books up here," I ventured.

"There was that one fellow at the Zionist camp near Magog," Eve corrected me. "He was reading the life of Ben-Gurion."

"Well, almost nobody."

A layover day at Sherbrooke gave us a chance to cool off, have some shoe repairs made, and catch up on laundry.

It had been in the middle and upper nineties for many days. The management of a large office building, in an effort to cool the build-

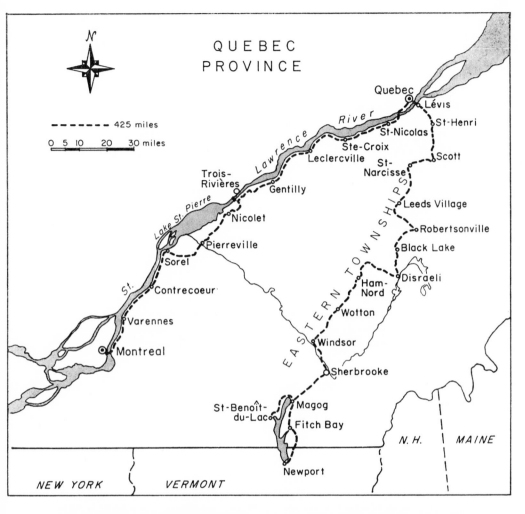

ing's interior, was pumping water out of the Magog River onto the roof, whence it drained back into the river. According to the pleasant young reporter who interviewed and photographed us for the local paper, the region had been without rain for a month, and some crops were already done for.

Unfazed by the heat were the bells of Sherbrooke's many churches, which rang constantly it seemed through our two nights in those incredibly hot hotel rooms. But we slept. During the day, we relaxed and puttered.

Amazingly renewed, we took to the road again, this time following the St.-François River first on one bank, then on the other.

Jim was wearing four pairs of socks "for more cushion." David had "accidentally" crushed the hated hat into a disgraceful mess. I now knew a little about the V⁹ chord. Eve was at last a teenager.

And it was still in the nineties.

A diet made up mostly of tomatoes and milkshakes carried us eighteen miles down the river to Windsor, a paper mill town. What from a distance had looked like a large hill turned out to be a mammoth pile of logs. The pleasant clear stream beside which we'd sat on a flat rock earlier in the day eating tomatoes was now a horrid, scummy body of water full of trash. The water that ran into our bathtub that night smelled foul like the air outdoors, and a tubful looked like rich tomato-beef broth.

Continuing to push in general north by northeast, we began to climb onto a great plateau, which brought with it twin blessings: a breeze now and then, and fine distant views. The heat was tapering off too, helped by showers.

In a shop at Windsor Jim had bought David a blue cap to replace the mutilated gray hat. And a few miles along he showed mercy, as a parent should be allowed to do occasionally.

"O.K., Dave, you win. Leave it here on this stump and maybe some kid who needs a cap will find it. The weather's going to be cooler from now on anyway. It's got to be. Danger of sunstroke is probably past."

"End of dumb cap," said Dave feelingly as he capped the stump.

"At your age I would've refused to wear it too," admitted the honest father.

Those fine distant views often showed us, across the rolling sea of farm and forest, a brilliantly shining aluminum church spire.

"What village is that?" someone would ask.

I'd look at the map. "St-Zacharie."

"We should make it in about twenty minutes. Let's have a milkshake there."

"Fine. I'm going to have strawberry for a change." In my heart I knew it would take at least an hour to get there, for I had the map.

After twenty minutes, the gleaming spire would still be all we could see of St-Zacharie, and it would take an hour or more to get there. Tiny though most of these villages were, they had huge, impressive churches thrusting bright silver *flèches* high into the sky like beacons on the plain.

Quebec was much more Catholic than France. Everywhere along the roadsides were peak-roofed shrines and calvaries—small, medium, and large—all with bouquets of real or artificial flowers. On street corners and in people's front yards there were shrines.

Certain saints were very popular, as evidenced by the names people gave their children. In the vicinity of St-Patrice, for example, Patrice was a common first name. Around St-Maxim, Maxims were rife. In churches, the figure of the local name saint usually rated the most candles, the most flowers.

Instead of the monuments to war dead to which we'd become accustomed on our walk across France, there was in most village squares a large statue of Jesus. Many of these statues had apparently been cast in the same mold; some were painted different colors or gilded. A few had electric halos. In our hotel rooms were crucifixes, pictures of saints, and bits of dry palm from Palm Sunday.

In public places there were placards showing Jesus, arms appealingly outspread, saying, "Ne me blasphémez pas" ("Do not blaspheme me"). On the door of a small grocery store, a metal plaque bore the legend, "Sainte Vièrge, bénissez notre entreprise" ("Holy Virgin, bless our business"). In shops of many kinds, rosaries and medals were for sale. For motorists, there was a St-Christophe, then the patron saint of travelers, which doubled as deodorizer. No car was without some kind of Christophe.

Regardless of our reaction to all this, we were grateful for those village churches with their tall aluminum spires. What we could see, we knew we could walk to.

After eight days on the road, came the revelation of a Great Truth. It was Saturday. The previous Saturday we'd slept at Fitch Bay in a private home. This second Saturday, we put down in a small undistinguished French hotel at the village of Wotton. After a fifteen-and-a-half-mile day, we were not exhausted but reasonably tired. Our thoughts were turning toward bed around eight o'clock, when one of the current Top Ten tunes boomed out from the bar, which, we now recollected, was about twenty feet from our rooms.

It began to dawn on us: the hotel was the weekend rumpus room for not only the village but the *chantiers de bûcherons* ("lumber camps") within a goodly radius.

Juke box, electric organ, tenor solos, community singing, shouts, laughter, slamming of doors, upsetting of furniture, breaking of glass—it all blended into a wholehearted uproar.

For five or six hours in our two rooms, we lay and listened. My thoughts spun out . . .

How great! The Old West still lives. . . . How fine! If it wouldn't put a crimp in their fun I'd like to get dressed again and go and join them. . . . How interesting! Wasn't De Quincy, on some walking trip, kept awake by revelers? We're in famous company. . . . How silly! You'd think they'd have had enough by now. . . . How inconsiderate! Keeping tired walking trippers awake till

all hours. . . . How disgusting! Getting so drunk on beer. . . .
How outrageous! Running a hotel like a Saturday brawl spot. . . .
How . . Z–z–z–z–z. . . .

FELLED BY FRIES

GREAT Truth Number Two about the Province of Quebec was
that due to Great Truth Number One (the "Saturdalian" spree), Sunday breakfast was just never ready when promised. Those who
weren't sleeping it off were at mass.

Eventually, fueled with cold boiled ham, poached eggs, and dry
(really dry again) cereal, we set out. Jim was wearing, yes, five pairs
of socks.

The children and I gorged ourselves at a roadside find of beautiful huckleberries while Jim, not a berry man, fretted.

Families drove past on their way back from mass. A lone couple
clip-clopped along in a horse-drawn buggy.

"Do you know what the Québecois say for 'to tie up' a horse?"
said Jim. "They say *amarrer,* to moor, like a boat."

"So I suppose instead of 'whoa' they say 'full speed astern,' " I
suggested.

"And 'full speed ahead' for 'giddap.' "

"And 'embark' for 'mount.' "

"And 'disembark' for 'dismount.' "

"And 'prow' for the horse's head."

"And 'stern' for his tail."

"And 'hold' for his belly."

"And 'deck' for his back."

"And 'shroud lines' for the reins."

"It all works out," Jim concluded, "because the French for
'saddle' is *selle* and that's obviously just a form of 'sail.' " The horse
and buggy disappeared over a hill about SSW.

No one ever stopped to speak with us, but when we met people
on foot or on bicycles or passed them working in their fields, we
engaged them in conversation as far as they would go. Most of them
could make nothing of people who walked by choice. A few, however, regarded us with grave approval. "C'est une promesse que vous
faîtes?" Well, if resolving to walk to Quebec and Montreal, come

heat wave or flood, and doing it, was a religious pilgrimage—yes, it was a *promesse*.

An approval more guarded yet was to be expressed a few days later by our second Scotsman. "Well," he burred when he learned our purpose, "therrrre's no harrrrm in it." He lived in a kind of Scottish enclave, a Gaelic island in a Gallic sea.

All the while in that Gallic sea, Jim was having a field day with the peculiarities of Canadian French.

"*Fah boo!*" he exulted. "Not *fait beau* but *fah boo!* How about that, Binkie!" The "eh" sound became "ah" and the "oh" sound became "oo." The vowels were being pronounced farther forward in the mouth. "Where will it end?" he wondered. "What will you get when you move 'oo' farther forward?"

Anyone who had heard us during the next fifty yards of our walk, as we experimented with that idea, would have taken us for lunatics.

Then there were the nasal effects. David remarked that their *oui* sounded like a quack from Donald Duck.

"These people were saying their *oui* before Donald Duck was even a duck egg," Jim informed him.

The French Canadian, we found, had pretty much discarded the distinction between the two kinds of floor: *plancher* ("floor of wood, tile, concrete," etc.) and *étage* ("second floor, ready-to-wear . . . third floor, lingerie," and so on). The Québecois simply called both kinds of floor *plancher*.

Then there were the words taken over from English, *la job,* and from the lumber industry, *le pulpe* and *la drave* (the "drive" of the logs downstream).

An old-fashioned usage that tickled Jim's funny bone was the rather elegant comment made by a clearly peasant-type woman. Clad in dirty apron, she was chasing a cow whose rump she belabored energetically with a stick. "Elle m'incommode," she explained to us. ("She inconveniences me.")

Cows, incidentally, were many now. Milk pails were upended over fence posts. Milk cans stood on small platforms by the roadside waiting for the co-op pickup, and always nearby was the two-wheeled handcart used to trundle the full cans to the platform and the empties back to the barn.

It was at Ham-Nord that I reached a reluctant conclusion about French Canadians—or at least French Canadian waitresses.

It had happened once or twice before, I thought. Here I distinctly observed it, at both dinner and breakfast. Ask for more water, and they bring instead of a pitcher, more glasses of water. Ask for more coffee, and they bring not the pot but more cups of coffee. As a housewife with a normal aversion to dishwashing, I put them down in my "book of nuts."

The following day was my birthday and, as on Eve's birthday, we were mapped for twenty-one miles. Not one but two stone Gabriels in front of the Ham-Nord church played me a silent fanfare on golden trumpets as we filed out of the village.

Even with five pairs of socks, Jim's feet were still bothering him. So he was not happy to learn, about midafternoon, that an alternate route would have saved us four miles. But he forgave me when he realized that had we taken it we'd have missed St-Fortunat, as quiet a little backwater as we were to encounter on the entire trip.

Hardly a soul was stirring in St-Fortunat. In the spacious plaza facing the enormous church, the figure of Christ with arms outspread wore a red painted cloak.

Between a modest dwelling and its family garage stood an elaborate glass-encased shrine, containing a replica of a celebrated Virgin statue that we would see more of later. The inscription read, "Cap-de-la-Madeleine, 1951." The family or some member(s) of it had evidently made a pilgrimage to that Canadian Lourdes, and, coming home, had erected the shrine to commemorate the pilgrimage, or perhaps even a cure.

Not far from the church was a tiny general store, where, some of us sitting on the steps of a ladder and the others standing, we refreshed ourselves with warmish pop brought up from the cellar through a trap door. Eve's face was a study in perplexity as she regarded the hodgepodge in showcases and on shelves: potatoes, gloves, tools, canned vegetables, hairnets, plastic toys, the inevitable St-Christophe medals and figurines.

Leaving St-Fortunat, we paused a moment on a small bridge over a tiny creek. A fish perhaps five inches long came to the surface, gave a few feeble flips and flops, seemed to gasp with its poor gills, and died there before our eyes.

I could not imagine why Jim's feet bothered him so. He was now convinced the solution lay not in more socks but different shoes. And when he saw Disraeli, our stop for the night, it seemed to promise well. "Any town that has two churches," he rejoiced, "must have a shoe store."

"Not necessarily," contributed an unfeeling member of the younger set.

In the sunset, Disraeli (the full name was St-Jacques-de-Disraeli, and wouldn't Queen Victoria's Jewish prime minister have laughed at that) was red and gold across a quiet lake. Teenage girls on a porch, singing to the accompaniment of a ukelele, paused briefly as we filed by on our way to the bridge and town.

One of the two "churches" turned out to be our hotel, white, with turret.

Its dining room having already closed, we had my birthday dinner at a diner. Eve and I, both born under the sign of Leo, seemed fated to have queer birthday celebrations.

I began my fiftieth year feeling fit. The children, however, were both violently indisposed, and some hours later I joined them. Of course—pop, ice cream bars, more pop, hamburgers, French fries, cake, all on top of twenty-one miles in broiling heat. What could we expect?

It might have been worse if we had sprinkled vinegar on our French fries as the Québecois do. Or if we'd eaten some of the pickled hard-boiled eggs or pickled corn on the cob that we kept seeing displayed like so many embryos in big jars of yellow gray brine. Expedition leader Jim, whose feet seemed to be all Achilles heel, was obviously our digestive better.

We took a two-day layover, and three of us thanked heaven and Disraeli for oatmeal gruel and tea.

SIGN OF INATTENTION

WHILE we recuperated, Jim invested in a pair of basketball shoes, keystone of his latest foot-comfort theory.

Disraeli wasn't a bad place to be sick. In these larger towns people were friendlier. Evenings, the streets were full of young people strolling in groups—groups of all boys or all girls, never mixed. A group of girls, who must have asked us a good hundred questions, informed us word had gone through town that we were walking around the world. Not quite, said we, and thanked them for the tribute.

Though we hadn't seen a copy of it, the Sherbrooke paper had by now published our picture and the interview with us. Perhaps it was from a careless reading of that article that our reputation as world walkers had sprung. Or from an illiterate reading, for the people continued to strike us as rather uneducated. Libraries continued to be conspicuously absent. Here in Disraeli I heard a man who had just bought a condolence card ask the shopkeeper to sign it for him. This was in contrast to France where, three years before, it had seemed to us that most people, including artisans and peasants, were fairly literate. Education in both France and Quebec has since been significantly upgraded.

In any event, because of the picture in the Sherbrooke *Daily Record,* the family of American hikers was now rather well known in the Eastern Townships. At one milkshake stop, a woman who recognized us and engaged us in conversation indicated she had gathered from the newspaper that Eve (aged thirteen years and nine days) was a famed cartoonist. On the strength of Eve's renown we ordered another round of milkshakes.

In order to reach overnight accommodations at walkable intervals, we were obliged now to do the two days from Disraeli to Robertsonville along the highway. Jim couldn't know for sure, therefore, how the basketball shoes were working out. " 'It's the everlasting 'ammer, 'ammer, 'ammer on the 'ard, 'ard 'ighway,' " he intoned as we arrived at Black Lake.

Asbestos is Quebec's top mineral resource, and Black Lake is one of Canada's big asbestos centers. That afternoon, we had passed an enormous open-pit asbestos mine. So huge was the manmade crater that railroad gondola cars in it looked like toys.

The town of Black Lake was neat and clean, cleaner than any mining town we'd ever seen—asbestos dust being white. The tap water, though, rivaled that of Windsor for color. Why, we never learned.

We were settling into our rooms when there came a long shrill siren, followed a few moments later by a terrific blast. They were dynamiting asbestos. This went on into the night, though not through the night: a siren and then a blast, then another siren and another blast.

But people who've walked most of the day, people who've learned to sleep through ever-tolling church bells, are not fazed by sirens and dynamite.

Having heard rumblings of a separatist movement in Quebec, we were on the lookout for signs and symptoms. This was, of course, before de Gaulle had made his unpolitic bid for the "liberation" of the province. Not until some years later was he to utter in Montreal those immortal, impolite, busybody words: "Vive le Québec libre!" ("Long live free Quebec!")

The Quebec Act of 1774 had guaranteed civil and linguistic rights to the French-speaking population, and from that time on these people had turned inward politically, away from both the French and the English.

During the summer of our trip, Maurice Duplessis, premier of Quebec and leader of the Union Nationale party, was at the height of his popularity. With his crusade for provincial autonomy, he had built what has been described as one of the most powerful and graft-ridden political machines Canada has ever known. When, about a week after our return home, he died following a series of strokes, the

Québecois filed past his bier by the thousands, weeping and praying for *"Le Chef."*

What separatist sentiment we observed (there were a few articles in provincial newspapers) indicated there was no drive for return to France, but merely for separation from the Dominion. Even so, we did meet one man on our thirty-five-day walking trip who openly favored separation. After talking with him, we concluded that, while Duplessis's movement might never succeed, it would help to insure the cultural survival of the French element.

(How near the truth we were remains to be seen. After cresting in the sixties separatism subsided, partly due to radical acts of violence which shocked and alienated, and partly due to conciliatory actions by Ottawa. Between 1970 and 1976, while Robert Bourassa was premier of Quebec, the province benefitted from: (1) a decrease in control of powerful corporations by English and English-Canadian interests, with corresponding increase in French-Canadian ownership; (2) an improving economy; (3) official bilingualism in the federal government; (4) a "language law" that over a five-year period is establishing French as the official provincial tongue; and (5) most importantly, growing acceptance by the rest of Canada of the idea of bilingual, bicultural accommodation. But in 1976 René Levesque's Parti Québecois, which advocates independence, won control of the provincial government. In August 1977, the provincial legislature passed a bill making French the official language of education, business, and government in Quebec. Premier Levesque promises a referendum on political separation, probably in the spring of 1979.)

But we did think one day that we'd happened on a nest of radical activists for the return of Quebec to France, when we saw what we carelessly took to be the French tricolor flying from a flagstaff at a crossroads.

"No," said Eve, who has always had a passion for flags and had memorized the U.N. flag chart. "The stripes of the French flag go up and down, not crosswise." This blue, white, and red ensign turned out to be that of St-Jean-Baptiste, patron saint of the province.

Once in a great while we would see portraits of the British royal couple displayed. But Elizabeth and Philip ran a poor third and fourth to first, the Holy Virgin, and second, Jesus. Quebec was loyal not to Paris, not to Buckingham Palace, somewhat to Ottawa, more to Quebec City, and perhaps most of all to Rome.

Despite its Scottish name, Robertsonville was thoroughly French and, as we realized about eight in the evening, thoroughly *québecois*. It was then that the Friday beer drinking started. To the accompaniment of music, yelling, door slamming, the driving up and driving away of cars, we concluded that asbestos workers must be blood brothers to lumbermen. Plus which, they must be on a five-day week and thus able to make merry on Friday as well as Saturday.

Sleep came finally, amid wistful thoughts of Black Lake with its sirens and dynamite blasts.

Striking northwest the next day on dirt road again, we found ourselves in a region reminiscent of the English Lake District. We talked of William and Dorothy Wordsworth, who in 1797 walked the Somerset coast with Coleridge. (Charming and impractical was this trio's scheme of jointly composing a poem while walking, to finance their tour. They gave it up as a group venture and Coleridge finished the poem alone. Thus, thanks to a walking tour, we have *The Rime of the Ancient Mariner.*)

There were woodland springs, made to order for our brief rest-and-snack stops. There were great stretches of pastureland to give us a sense of space, with lakes that smiled from dark green frames. A few wispy carefree clouds strewed an azure sky, and oodles of blueberries grew by the wayside. The road—it was almost exclusively ours, so sparse was travel—seemed to have been laid out not by some quadrant-and-slide-rule surveyor, but by a poet who cared for fine prospects, even at the cost of a bit more distance or a bit more climb.

About midway in this perfect seventeen-mile day was Kinnears Mills, ideally located for refilling our canteens. Three churches graced the main street of the pocket-size hamlet: a French Catholic church, an Anglican church, and a Scottish (Candlish) church.

"Why don't they get together," asked David, "the way they do in some of those French villages?" He was referring to the Alsatian villages in which Catholics and Protestants use the same church at different hours. Why not?

Kinnears Mills will live in our memory not only for its three churches, but for a delightful soft drink which we first tasted there: *bière d'épinette,* made from spruce.

A few feet short of our country hotel at Leeds Village (St-Jacques-de-Leeds) I was so busy reading the sign on a blacksmith shop across the road that I missed my footing at the curb and sprawled headlong. As usual in such circumstances, Jim was torn between concern and disgust. He gathered me up and, seeing that I was in shock, gave me water from his canteen. I assured him I had nothing worse than a badly bruised knee. His look said, "People who are said to be walking around the world, and can't even negotiate a simple curb!"

AFTER WOLFE,
YOUNGS AT THE DOOR

DOCTOR Jim prescribed gin and water before dinner and the patient submitted willingly to the treatment, for the knee was painful.

The night, being Saturday, was noisy. All night, outside our window, the statue of Jesus was floodlighted. I know because I was awake on and off till dawn.

According to the lady who the night before had sold us some bread and cheese for the road, the first mass would be at seven-thirty, and she assured us there would be *beaucoup de places* (plenty of seats). But, she'd said, if we were planning to go to the nine-thirty *messe* we'd find all the places taken. She didn't mention a six o'clock mass, but the bells did—at, it seemed, arm's length from our heads.

So, in our usual heavy-eyed Sunday morning condition, we waited, famished, while the management attended seven-thirty mass. Our general grumpiness vanished when, after the long-delayed breakfast of cold-storage eggs, the four of us found ourselves brushing our teeth in concert around a single wash basin. Lather and laughter brightened us up for the twenty miles ahead.

Jim's Disraeli basketball shoes were getting a real test. The map hereabouts had indicated our favorite kind of surface, dirt, but the provincial government had gotten there first with truckloads of coarse sharp gravel. Though footsore, Jim continued optimistic. "I really think I've got an unbeatable combination in the five pairs of socks and the basketball shoes," he insisted. . . . "If it weren't for this gravel, I'd be walking on air. . . . Some day it'll revolutionize outdoor footwear. . . . I'll call it 'the floating foot!' "

I *would* choose that gravelly twenty-mile day to have a falling out with the map. Unlike road signs in France, which usually indicate not only direction but distance down to the last tenth of a kilometer, the Quebec signs almost never concerned themselves with the how far. So when, at eight that evening after a long hot Sunday on gravel, we reached the wee hamlet of St-Narcisse, Jim wasn't the only footsore one. I calculated we'd walked not twenty but twenty-three miles. Tempering their ire at mapper Mama, the others confessed to some pride in having set a new family record.

The official tourist accommodations list called it the "Hôtel Laboureur, St-Narcisse." In reality it was the home of M. *et Mme* Laboureur, with the upstairs available to travelers. Of the three upstairs bedrooms, we took two. The other remained unoccupied, and we had, it appeared, exclusive use of the bathroom.

Though his family name, Laboureur ("plowman"), indicated

agricultural ancestry, Monsieur had risen to the petite bourgeoisie. He was, in fact, an end product of a social trend.

The seventeenth-century French settlers had, many of them, received land tenure from Louis XIV. The grant was often only a narrow strip of land with a small river frontage. After the Treaty of Paris, which ended the Seven Years War in 1763 and established British possession of Canada, the Province of Quebec continued strongly conservative and agrarian, with dual leadership from the clergy and these seigniorial landholders. In succeeding decades it was common for such a farmer to turn to one of the professions, becoming a notary, a lawyer, a teacher, or the like. M. Laboureur was a licensed *adjutant,* or justice of the peace.

It was the Monsieur Laboureurs who spearheaded the French faction's long and still-continuing fight against the Scottish and English mercantile interests for preservation of the French language and culture.

As for Madame Laboureur, she was a pleasant housewife and *mère de famille.* Though she and her fellow housewives had been granted federal suffrage two years before American women had won theirs, I suspect her vote usually mirrored Monsieur's. What mattered more to us at the time, she was an excellent home cook.

They had expected us for the night because we'd telephoned a reservation. But when it got late they'd given us up. So there was a wait while Madame Laboureur fired up the stove again a little after eight and began boiling potatoes, heating soup, fixing hamburgers and gravy, slicing big Bermuda onions onto lettuce, and washing the *bleuets* for dessert. The kitchen was warm and cosy but she insisted on serving us, at long last, in the dining room.

Except for a few bizarre tastes like pickled corn on the cob, French-Canadian cuisine differs little from American cooking. Madame Laboureur's home-cooked meal, typical of what we got most of the time, was excellent fare.

Hunger appeased, we had time, before going upstairs, to look more closely at the framed items on the dining room walls: a picture of Monsieur in his jurist robe; his license; a picture of (in all likelihood) his or Madame's sister in her nun's habit; and the family tree. We were much moved by the group commencement picture, with somewhere in it the child who was their pride.

"Bonne nuit, Madame. Bonne nuit, Monsieur." We bade them goodnight and climbed wearily up to bed.

Rain dogged us now for a couple of days but we pushed on, excited by our nearness to the city of Quebec. The two ponchos were excellent to sit on in the wet grass for between-showers snacks.

Occasionally we stopped in some cafe for tea to warm us. Once, desperately cold and wet, we prevailed upon a housewife to make us some tea and accept our money for it. She was a gracious lady, warm and unsuspicious—unlike the "closed" rural folk—and a herald of the more sophisticated and outgoing metropolitan area we were approaching.

Another altogether outgoing and helpful person in this pre–Quebec City region was the lady who rescued my letter. I mailed a letter in a slot marked *poste,* as one might be expected to do, and she rushed out of her shop.

"Madame, madame! On n'en sert plus!" ("One no longer uses it. Wait!") "Attendez!" She disappeared, returned with two table knives, and cleverly fished out the truant missive.

"Why doesn't she just board up the slot?" suggested David as we pressed on. "Or paint over the word *poste?* It would save her a lot of trouble."

"I suspect," commented Jim, "that the drama of these little situations relieves the monotony of life in St-Bernard."

Appropriate to the depressing weather were the crosses and calvaries along the way. Whereas in France a simple cross usually sufficed, here in French Canada there was an insistence on the grim details of the Crucifixion.

The crown of thorns was depicted, realistically hanging from the intersection of the cross. The three spikes used to nail Jesus' hands and feet to the cross were there, and the mocking sign INRI. Occasionally a length of cloth was draped over the cross. Most conspicuous of all was the ladder, like a diagonal accent mark.

Seeing these rather morbid calvaries all through the Eastern Townships, we had reminded the children of the story of Joseph of Arimathea and his recovery of the body.

"But," said Eve, "that ladder is just too short and flimsy for bringing a body down." Now, there was a practical young girl.

After fifteen days of walking plus three days of layover, we were 227 miles from our rainy departure at Newport, Vermont. The St. Lawrence River and Quebec City were but 12 miles distant, an easy day's walk.

As though preparing for our arrival, the weather cleared. We walked in high spirits in the usual order: first Jim, then Dave, then Eve, then Mama. We laughed and joked; we sang an occasional song and made plans for our layover in Quebec.

From our Gaspé trip six years before, we all of course remembered the huge Chateau Frontenac Hotel, though we hadn't stayed in it. About noon Dave descried its tall green roof against the horizon and let out a whoop. "There's the Frontenac! There's Quebec! I saw it first!"

Ferryboats were shuttling the St. Lawrence between Quebec and, on our shore, Lévis. It was obvious that service was frequent. We could be across in no time.

But the commander lined us up and looked us over—a ragtag company indeed. After two days of walking in the rain, our clothes were stained and rumpled. Until that morning, they hadn't been really dry for some fifty-six hours.

"Mama," he scolded, "your jacket looks as though you'd slept in it."

"I have. Remember? To keep warm."

The three of us who weren't wearing basketball shoes needed heel and toe plates. Our hair was dirty. The commander himself needed a haircut.

This was no way to take Quebec, he decided.

And so Lévis—historic and interesting in its own right, but over-shadowed by the more glamorous city across the river—won the dubious honor of providing bed, board, and cleanup to four Iowa tramps.

We had all afternoon and evening to launder, to have shoe repairs, to shower, to shampoo. The drip-dries hanging in the shower would be fresh and clean to don the next day.

True, the people of that busy city across the river could not care less whether, stepping off the ferryboat in the morning, we were clean or dirty, shampooed or unshampooed. True, the personnel at the modest hotel where we had reserved rooms would have other concerns than whether or not our heels were run down.

Still, it was something to have walked from the United States to a Canadian provincial capital, and a sense of fitness demanded "dress uniform."

For Jim's haircut, I seated him facing the window so he could contemplate the imposing Quebec skyline in the moonlight.

"It was two hundred years ago next month that the British took Quebec," I informed my tonsorial client. "They bombarded the city from here."

"Unsucessfully," he added. "And did you know that one factor in Wolfe's success was his knowledge of French?

"Children," he called, "if General Wolfe hadn't perfected his French, Quebec might still belong to France!"

"Sit still," I chided, "if you don't want to enter the city looking like an advertisement for bargain day at the barber college."

AN OLD LOVE AFFAIR

QUEBEC CITY was like meeting a former sweetheart—flashes of pleasure at things recognized and beloved; starts of surprise at things not known before; faint unnamed regret at the impossibility of following to its conclusion every strand once held in the hand.

It had been six years since, en route to Gaspé, we'd spent time in Quebec, the most Old World city in the New World. Dufferin Terrace was still there: that dramatic boardwalk overlooking the lower city and the St. Lawrence two hundred feet below. As before, I wondered how all those people could sit there so calmly, reading or dozing or looking at each other. Why weren't they excited about the view of Lévis across the river, about the throng of vessels large and small coming and going on the great waterway at their feet, about the incredible Chateau Frontenac with its verdigris roofing, its towers and turrets and dormers?

As before, we took a drive in a calèche. Now, however, we were a much heavier load, and we all felt twinges of guilt when the poor horse had to drag us up cobbled streets that were as steep as they were picturesque.

As before, we rambled the ramparts and examined the cannon. At the citadel, with a handful of other tourists, we watched the changing of the guard. The officers were clad in strictly British uniforms of scarlet cloth, brass buttons, and tall fur caps. How odd it was to hear them barking their orders in French! We were shown the mascot of the guard, a royal billy goat with gilded horns and hoofs, and I wished they hadn't told us that he's bred with a provincial nanny to provide kid gloves for the officers.

At the wax museum, like so many other gullible visitors, we asked a question of a guard who was made of wax. But in a way we turned the tables. A few minutes later Jim whispered something to Dave and they took their places on a bench and sat motionless until a sightseeing couple stopped, searched their catalog for information about the strange-looking man and boy, and finally reacted with both amusement and annoyance when our pranksters stood up and walked away.

A thunderstorm cleared just in time for us to take a cruise on the St. Lawrence, and it was hard to say whether the cruise itself was more interesting—with its bridges, its river traffic, its view of Montmorency Falls, its wind and spray—or the conversation of the tour guide. We were almost the only passengers, and he willingly told us his life story, which included time spent living among Eskimos in the Arctic while in the Winter Warfare Service of the Canadian Army.

We couldn't resist a return visit to the Champ de Bataille. This time, instead of meeting with disaster brought on by my having walked under a ladder, we met a delightful group of young Jewish hitchhikers, American and Canadian. We'd made their acquaintance days earlier at Camp Kissoufim (Camp Yearning). After giving them a map which they needed and some advice which they probably didn't need, we parted from them, and I heard them start speaking Hebrew at once.

Wandering through a market in the lower town, we saw blood for sale in blocks and hurried on squeamishly. Yes, Quebec is Old World.

Two things I kept wondering about. There was the church of Notre Dame des Victoires. It was named in commemoration of military engagements in 1690 and 1711, both of which were defeats. History is indeed often a matter of perspective.

The other thing that bothered me was the provincial motto, *"Je me souviens"* ("I remember"). Who remembers what? No reference book on Quebec history, no book on heraldry has yielded me a clue, nor did the provincial government ever reply to my inquiry. Queen Elizabeth II herself became a party to the mystery when, visting Canada later on, she quoted the motto without elucidating.

Jim and I had been married twenty-two years. It called for a celebration and at the festive dinner it was easy enough to decide that yes, we would continue to Montreal. We had the money, if we would watch it closely. We had the time—just barely. Certainly we had the know-how. It had really been just a pretense, that business of "We'll see when we get to Quebec." I don't think any of us ever thought for a moment that we would finish the walking trip at Quebec.

From the Department of Forestry I was able to secure excellent large-scale maps which told us not only more about where we were going but more about where we'd been. At once I lined up reservations for the first few nights of our southwest bound trek up the St. Lawrence.

The children and I had acquired much needed toe and heel plates and Jim had bought a new pair of basketball shoes. He was now certain that with a better fit, his feet would indeed "float."

All that was needed was a formal leave taking. "What shall we do to say goodby to Quebec?" he asked.

"Let's go back to that drug store where I saw the sparklers and get some," replied David without hesitation.

"Let's go down to the lower city and come up in the *ascenseur* again," said Eve.

"I'd like to take a last walk on Dufferin Terrace," said I.

"And I," said Jim, "would like to see if we can find that place where we stayed when we were here before."

We did it all. Sparklers, unavailable at home, were bought and stowed in David's knapsack. It was easy to walk down to the lower city and board the municipal elevator which lifted us two hundred feet straight up the bluff. It let us out on Dufferin Terrace and once more I was wishing I could thank Lord Durham, who had conceived this peerless boardwalk, surely one of the most unforgettable prospect points in the wide world. And finally there was Jim, with his superb memory and sure instinct for location, leading us unerringly to the modest rooming house where we'd stayed six years before.

UPSTREAM AND UPSET

TWO roads follow the St. Lawrence upstream, southwest, from Quebec to Montreal. We let the motorists have the fine new high-speed highway and took the little-used old road along the south shore.

Huge ocean liners flying the flags of faraway nations were steaming in both directions on the three-quarter-mile-wide river. Behind them, like ducklings in flotilla behind mama ducks, small sturdy lumber schooners plied their ways, their decks piled high with future telephone poles, future newsprint, future charcoal briquets. Each of these schooners, we learned, had been blessed by a priest before putting out on its first voyage. Some of them had been constructed by villagers as a communal project.

Seven miles upstream from Quebec, in a drizzle that had an all day air about it, we took the pedestrian path across the Quebec Bridge and found something to be glad about. It was great not to be engaged in work like engineering, where an error could cost lives. The Quebec Bridge had collapsed during building, not once but twice.

It was a rainy Sunday, too rainy-hazy to see much. The old road paralleled the river, close enough for us to hear the boats whistling at each other through the blur.

Late in the afternoon as the sun came out and began to raise a fine steam from the land, I discovered to my shame that I'd reserved motel rooms several miles off our route. It was a matter of nomenclature, I apologized, a confusion between St-Nicolas village and St-Nicolas parish. Cold, wet, and tired, the other three couldn't have cared less how it had happened.

In the village we decided to stop at a charming-looking old hotel and telephone a cancellation to the motel. However, the proprietors of the hotel had seen fit to close down for the day and go to Montreal. *Hm! To think that all these years Jim and I had resisted an urge to go into the hotel business because it would tie us down.*

In leisurely Sunday mood St-Nicolas folk were standing about in the street, or rocking on front porches, chatting together and eyeing the four quaint Americans in their midst. We discussed our plight at some length with a couple of groups, and finally a friendly fellow, who must have felt somewhat ashamed for those irresponsible hotel-keepers, led us to a house where he thought we might get rooms for the night. Alas, *pensionnaires* had them all.

By now it was pretty late to start walking the six miles to the motel.

There must have been at least half a dozen people in St-Nicolas who owned cars, half a dozen people who could have been hired to drive us those six miles. But in that game of Russian roulette, we chose the chamber with the cartridge: a harmless-looking *habitant* with a car of fairly recent vintage.

Would we mind if his wife came along, our chauffeur asked in French. Of course not.

The four of us sat in back. For a French-Canadian *char* this was nothing unusual; four was about minimum rear-seat load. He took the wheel, Madame got in beside him. He drove perhaps five hundred yards out of the village, pulled up at the roadside, and went around to Madame's side. She slid her ample self under the wheel.

"Ma femme apprend à conduire," he told us pleasantly "C'est une bonne opportunité pour de l'expérience." ("My wife is learning to drive. It is a good opportunity for experience.") "Vous n'avez pas d'objection?" Not at all, no objection, we assured him gallantly.

All went pretty well for a few feet, until Madame swerved grandly to avoid a dead cat. Monsieur grabbed the wheel just before we went into the ditch. She called him two or three names which, uttered in tender tones, might have passed in Paris for terms of endearment. But this was French Canada, and the tones weren't tender, no. We cowered in back.

Monsieur now reminded her that this was Sunday and that all the fools of the province would be on the highway we were approaching. She must remain calm. He who is calm, he philosophized, wins the day.

She found this *très amusant*. He was telling her to be calm! She was as calm as the bottom of the sea. It was he who—and with that she swung onto the highway in front of a gasoline truck, honking her horn at it after it had narrowly missed us. The driver honked back.

"Écoutez, Albert! Qu'il est impoli! Le fripon!" ("Listen to that! How rude! The rascal!")

And so it went, breathtakingly, for nearly six miles along the highway to the motel. Every now and then Monsieur would turn full around to us with lame jokes about Madame's ineptitude. She would turn to him and call him French-Canadian names, letting go of the wheel to illustrate her meaning. We would turn pale.

The next morning the motel manager gave us a lift back to St-Nicolas to pick up our trail where we had left it.

Now for four days we walked along the south bank of the St. Lawrence. Spendid fields of grain grew out to the steep dropoff of the shore. Here and there a white tower, a landlocked lighthouse, stood in the midst of a wheat field as a triangulation point for river navigators. In pastures, old lard kettles were used as watering troughs. In an occasional farmyard, a well sweep flung its old-time shape against the sky.

Periodically, where a tributary river emptied into the St. Lawrence, the land dipped to a cosy cove complete with village and church. (One such village, complete also with general store that furnished Jim with his next pair of basketball shoes, fell heir to the ones he discarded.)

A new note was struck by lush estates, some of them a bit down at the heel, on village outskirts. Their pretentious mansions were set in parklike grounds where mossy, crumbly pedestals supported mossy, crumbly statuary. Some had tennis courts; others, croquet courts. Most had small private chapels, usually of brick and with locked doors—very different from the hospitable kind of shrine-on-a-post-with-a-place-to-kneel which we'd seen along waysides in the Eastern Townships.

There was rain or mist on and off those four days, with invisible seagulls sometimes screaming above us. Then it would clear, and like a vision in some corny but wonderful stage spectacle, there would be an elegant, shapely ocean liner on the blue gray river, with gay white waves curling away from its bow. Or near at hand there'd be a long neat pile of firewood, thatched over with slabs of birch bark, or a stooped *vieillard* picking his yearly crop of tobacco leaves in the small field dedicated to satisfaction of his petty vice. Or a man feeding pigs out of pails hanging from a yoke over his shoulders, or even, occasionally, way beyond the river, the Laurentian Mountains, clothed in the blue haze of miles.

And so we progressed upstream, with good moments (many) and bad. A good one was when we read a small sign on the lawn of some Catholic institution. *Il Faut Aimer le Gazon*, it said. ("It is necessary to love the grass.") How much nicer than Keep Off!

An immortal bad moment was the instant when a fried egg set before Eve was discovered to harbor somebody's chewing gum. Because the word *yech* had not yet come into the language, poor Eve was unable to give adequate expression to her feelings.

A funeral knell was sounding from the church tower in Ste-Croix, and from the church door the undertaker was emerging in his high silk hat.

With part of the hearse in the foreground and the church steps in the background, he would have made an excellent picture. Instinctively I reached for my camera, held it to my eye, focused—and decided it would be in bad taste to take the picture. The camera went back into its case.

A little while later, as we were walking the road beyond Ste-Croix in our usual formation, me bringing up the rear, I happened to glance back. Following us on foot at some distance was a man in clerical garb. *The priest from Ste-Croix,* I thought, *pursuing us to scold me for photographing a funeral! Maybe there's even a law against it.*

I said nothing to the others, and we continued at our leisurely pace. Surreptitiously I glanced back again. He was gaining on us, with quick and purposeful step. *Could I convince him that I had not actually pressed the shutter button?*

Now I definitely heard footsteps behind me. Shame engulfed me. *How could I have even thought of doing such a tasteless thing?*

PULP AND POMP

THE face that looked out from under the stiff black broadbrim was not a scowling one. Nor was it French-Canadian.

Cyrille Pyon Eul, South Korean divinity student, beamed a benevolent smile as he returned my *bonjour* and joined our ranks. For the next few miles he walked sometimes beside one of us, sometimes beside another.

A student at the Grand Séminaire in Quebec City, he was spending his summer holiday at a friend's farm. Each morning he walked to Ste-Croix for mass, and he was now on his way back to the farm.

Orphaned early in the Korean War, he had somehow survived walking two hundred miles, alone, aged about ten, in winter, to a relief station. And we thought we'd done something—at the end of a well-fed well-shod, well-sheltered summer trip!

Now he had one more year of studies at the seminary before he would be a fully ordained priest and return to Korea to work under a French bishop there.

Walking along, and later as we all sat in a roadside ditch where he shared our fruit and milk, we discussed many things with this intelligent, handsome, pleasant young Korean. He had pertinent, open-minded questions to ask regarding the science of semantics, to which we'd recently had an exciting introduction through S. I. Hayakawa's *Language in Thought and Action.* He knew of Rhee yil Sun, a Korean doctor who had worked in leper care with the man I so admired, Dr. Albert Schweitzer. Cyrille Eul eagerly discussed Schweitzer's philosophy, his own and new trends in philosophy and theology.

An after-dinner walk one evening introduced us to the "bathing machine"—a tiny cabin that can be carried like a sedan chair by means of two shafts. Painted all the hues of the rainbow, the cabins were lined up in a colorful row against the bank on the river beach. People of the St. Lawrence villages did not as yet believe in donning swim suits at home to walk the short distance to the water.

Beside a pair of rusty bitts on an old ferry jetty the four of us sat down to watch the sun set across the river and the lights come on in the village over there. A French-Canadian family came ashore after an outing on the river. In tone, their talk was high pitched and excited sounding; in content, it was trivial and homely, like the talk of a billion other families. Their dog barked and capered. The rowboat's bottom complained and scraped over the rocks as they beached it. Chalk up another unforgettable moment.

At Magog we had laughed about the closet with a bathtub in it. At Lévis, we had laughed, perhaps a little bitterly, to learn that in a really modern first-class hotel where there were rooms with showers galore, there was not one room with its own toilet. At Gentilly now, we laughed with pure delight. The advertisements had said "Spacious rooms with bath and toilet." It was literally true: toilet and full-size bathtub were right in the bedroom. No curtain, no screen, just a toilet and tub, right there, baldly, in the bedroom. Let no man say that life in the Province of Quebec is standardized.

Wood is the lifeblood of Quebec, Canada's number one province in forest industry. Every farmyard had its pile of cordwood. In late summer the woodpiles were beginning to lengthen as the men of the family worked at cutting a winter's supply. Evenings and early mornings, blue gray tails of smoke ascended from chimneys, perfuming the air.

On the St. Lawrence, the lumber schooners plied their busy courses, and, increasingly now, there were the pulp mills with their mountains of small logs, their tall stacks gushing waste-product smoke. Quebec produces more than half of Canada's vast output of newsprint.

"How can it be," I wondered aloud, "that fresh-cut wood smells so good, and wood pulp smells so bad?"

It was like coffee, Jim said. Fresh-ground coffee had a heavenly perfume and "coffee grounds smell like hell."

"Or it's like vanilla," offered David. "It smells wonderful and tastes terrible."

"Not like salt-rising bread," added Eve. "It smells terrible and tastes wonderful." That reminded us we were hungry, and we stopped for a quick snack.

Appropriately in this lumber country, we noticed many king-size Paul Bunyanish men. So we ought not to have been too startled to learn from the plaque on a boulder the size of an overstuffed armchair that the boulder had been moved, unaided, by one Modeste Mailhot, who stood seven feet four inches and weighed more than six hundred pounds.

Modeste's line had not died out, for the name Mailhot appeared on several mailboxes thereabouts. We took great care not to step on Mailhot property, nor give possible offense in any other way.

We were nearing Trois-Rivières (Three Rivers) Canada's foremost pulp center. Near Trois-Rivières is Cap-de-la-Madeleine, a pilgrimage spot less well known to tourists than Ste-Anne-de-Beaupré but so venerated by Catholics that a million and a half pilgrims visit the Cap yearly. At St-Fortunat we'd seen a shrine-replica of the miraculous statue of Notre-Dame-du-Très-Saint-Rosaire. People had even taken us for Cap pilgrims.

Now, some five miles before reaching Trois-Rivières, we sighted the exotic hexagonal dome of an enormous basilica under construction at Cap-de-la-Madeleine.

A small auto ferry took us from Ste-Angèle-de-Laval to Trois-Rivières, a city about the size of Sherbrooke and even more French speaking—95 percent. One of the earliest settlements in Quebec, Trois-Rivières is not really named for three rivers but for one, the St-Maurice, which here divides around two sizable islands to empty into the St. Lawrence by three mouths. The Duplessis Bridge across one of its mouths had collapsed eight years before when a thirty-below-zero cold snap "brittle-ized" its steel.

Trois-Rivières was on our itinerary as a layover place for a visit to Cap-de-la-Madeleine and for the regular rest and freshening up.

Covering many many acres along the north shore of the St. Lawrence, Cap-de-la-Madeleine was a complex of numerous buildings, shrines, and sacred sites. Mass was being said when we entered the chief sanctuary, over whose altar stood the miraculous statue of Notre-Dame-du-Très-Saint-Rosaire. This was the statue which, we were told, had caused the St. Lawrence to freeze over for a single day in 1897, so that horse-drawn sleds could be brought across the river with stone for a new chapel. Other miracles, including many cures, were credited to the statue; crutches, canes, braces, and plaques of *reconnaissance* ("gratitude") lined the sanctuary walls.

A replica of the miraculous statue, known as the "pilgrim statue," had recently returned to the Cap after years of travel throughout the Dominion, and was housed in a different building. It must have been that statue which had passed ahead of us on the Gaspé coast six years earlier. The pilgrim statue was the object of veneration nearly equal to that enjoyed by the authentic statue. (David and Eve, schooled in basic hygiene, were amazed to see people kissing its feet and even holding small children up to kiss them.)

Dominating the entire area was the mammoth basilica whose hexagonal roof we had sighted from afar, a colossus still under construction.

We found the pomp and splendor of Cap-de-la-Madeleine in vivid contrast to the simplicity of St-Benoît-du-Lac, where life was made up of labor, music, prayer, and meditation—and in vivid contrast to the gentle serenity of Cyrille Pyon Eul.

FOUR ON A VOW

THE layover at Trois-Rivières produced some advance in our assorted projects, as had our other layovers. Eve had diligently practiced on her oboe reed. Dave had improved his speed at Morse code. Jim had added a new and flavorful bit to his catalog of French-Canadian pronunciations: *Paws (pas) ici* ("not here"). I had started the general review exercises at the back of the music theory text.

Least astonishing of all, Jim had discarded another pair of shoes, this time in favor of something that had caught his eye in a Trois-Rivières shop window. Declared he ever hopefully: "This will make all the difference. I predict you'll all be converted to this type of footgear." After three pairs of basketball shoes he had come full circle to a leather shoe again, this one with heavy sponge-rubber sole.

More than a hundred miles lay between us and Montreal. Our exchequer was getting slim. At home, school would be opening soon. We needed to get to Montreal for an August 28 train departure. That gave us five and a half days for the 105 miles.

Equipped with his handsome, rather orange shoes, the head of the family felt nothing could stop us now—not even the fact that we were setting out short on sleep again. For pulp center Trois-Rivières held to the lumber tradition. Like Wotton on Saturday night, like Leeds Village on Saturday night, Trois-Rivières had not slept till nearly dawn on Sunday.

Breakfast at seven? Breakfast at all on Sunday? *Paws ici,* said the hotel. We packed up, paid, and packed off for the bus depot, where we thought someone might be stirring at the lunch counter. At eight-fifteen, they were just making the coffee.

"Mama," whispered Eve, "she's putting salt in the coffee!" It was true.

"You're the salt in my coffee," I sang softly to Jim.

"You're the cream in my stew."

"You will always be my necessity—"

"I'd be lost without you."

The children blushed for their absurd parents, who were always harking back to some dumb popular song of the twenties or thirties.

Even the relatively deserted south bank of the St. Lawrence became somewhat hectic later in the morning as carloads of the devout passed us en route to or from mass. At the wheel, Papa; at his side in her best black, Mama; on her lap, at her sides, and throughout the rear, *les enfants*—coated, buttoned, gloved, shined, brushed, combed, curled, and all but spilling out the windows.

Someone had told us that Quebec Province had the highest birth rate on the continent and that in Quebec (and Newfoundland) every divorce had to be sanctioned by an Act of Parliament. The institution of the family was evidently in no danger here. (Quebec's birth rate is now down to almost lowest on the continent, and the provincial government is fighting the trend by paying subsidies to large families.)

Most of the youths we saw were good looking, broad shouldered, vigorous, manly, and of generous height—despite the fact that they seemed to start smoking soon after they learned to walk.

Nicolet, our first overnight stop after Trois-Rivières, presented a forbidding aspect. It was a Marian Center, seat of a diocese and location of a Catholic seminary, and consisted mainly of great stone buildings in large grounds—all quite deserted in the vacation period.

Ah, we thought, *a quiet town, a good sleep!*

But, come Sunday nightfall, Nicolet roused itself to rival Saturday night in the rowdiest lumber town. This was not only annoying but mystifying because, as the hotel manager told us, liquor was not sold in Nicolet on Sunday. He swayed precariously as he said it.

Consequently, Monday morning in Nicolet was like Sunday morning elsewhere, breakfast for travelers being farthest from *hôteliers'* thoughts. A *petit déjeuner* (too *petit*) rustled up at a tiny cafe on the town square raised our spirits from "terrible" to "awful," and we set out in raincoats and ponchos to do seventeen miles under ceiling zero.

Instead of the customary milkshake stops, it was tea stops and a soup stop. New shoes notwithstanding, Jim's feet still bothered him—the left one in particular.

But the closer we got to Montreal, the more determined we were to walk every step of the way. The thing was beginning to assume almost the character of a religious commitment, a *promesse*.

Wet, cold, and bedraggled, we filed into Pierreville and settled ourselves in the Hôtel Manoir, literally an old manor. Suddenly it was as though we were truly someone's guests, as we had been that lucky day in France when Colonel Mills had found us at Fresne-le-Plan. Our two rooms were clean and charmingly furnished. Through an open door, as we rested and dried out, wonderful dinner smells drifted up to us.

The dining room was evidently just as it had been when it served as mealtime gathering place for the gracious well-to-do family which was now making the best of lean times. The oak table, chairs, and buffet shone. A large crystal chandelier shimmered above us. Knives, forks, and spoons were of sterling. Extra spoons hung from a cut-glass rack in the center of the table. More cut glass sparkled on the buffet. Heavy drapes hung at the windows. The pictures on the walls were not cheap reproductions but oil paintings in good taste.

Acutely conscious of the personal nature of the establishment, we spoke in muted tones while eating an excellent meal—cooked, no doubt, by a lady who'd had to learn cooking in middle age. Hungry though we were after seventeen miles on the road, bites were smaller than usual. Glassware and silver were handled quietly and carefully. We asked for things that ordinarily we'd have seized with boarding-house reach.

A small room off the dining room still served as music room, and in it stood an old upright piano with glass front, so the hammers could be seen striking the strings. There, after dinner, the lady who had served us sat down and played that top hit of our newlywed days, "Mexicali Rose." And so to bed, pondering the whereabouts of the snows of 1937 and other yesteryears.

Paradoxically, though Montreal was now only about sixty-five miles distant and we were definitely aware of suburban homes and metropolitan traffic, thatch-roofed barns suddenly appeared. But, metropolis or no metropolis, pasteurized milk was still a sometimes thing. Slowly, but slowly, the good Louis Pasteur's enlightenment was creeping over the face of Quebec.

Sorel, at the point where the Richelieu River empties into the St. Lawrence, offered us a new olfactory experience. Piles of sulfur waiting to be loaded at the river docks gave off a sickening smell rather like that of escaping gas. Sorelians, like the inhabitants of the ill-smelling pulp towns, went about their business as though they lacked noses.

From Sorel Jim called Montreal and confirmed our Pullman reservations, committing us to get to the Central Station by three o'clock Friday afternoon. That meant forty-four and a half miles to walk, and Wednesday, Thursday, and part of Friday to do it in.

There's no off-the-beaten-path route to enter a city the size of Montreal. We knew there would be the usual big-city irritants—traffic, smoke, noise, tension.

On the drawbridge over the Richelieu River just out of Sorel, the four of us shook hands all around and promised that, come what might, between that moment and train time Friday we'd be good sports.

"I'll be glad when this dumb trip is over," David summarized.

"So will my left foot," said Jim.

THE CRUNCH

TO make things jollier, the first of our last three days started off with thunder, lightning, wind, and downpour. Along with Thor, Vulcan was busy: we could see molten metal being poured in a St-Joseph foundry. On and off all day, National Defence Proving Ground cannons roared past us on great trucks.

At last the weather cleared, and, just when the commuter traffic to Montreal was beginning to get thick, we were provided with a bicycle path on which to walk in safety and comparative quiet.

"If this keeps up clear to Montreal," said Jim, "it'll be as easy as duck soup."

It won't keep up, said something old and cynical within me. Remembering the handshakes on the Richelieu drawbridge, I held my peace.

This Canadian suburb that had thought of everything, even a bike path, had not overlooked waste disposal. It was garbage-collection day, and our pace along the bike path was perfectly synchronized with the stop-and-go pace of the foul-smelling truck.

"Let's hurry and get ahead of it." We tried. It overtook us.

"Let's slow down and let it get ahead of us." It made an extra-long stop and we overtook it.

"Let's stop at the next shady spot and have a snack." We did. Ah! It passed us and got out of smell. Rising to go on, we discovered we'd been sitting in poison ivy. The bike path petered out.

A couple of milkshake stops later, poison ivy, garbage, and commuter traffic were forgotten. For between us and the St. Lawrence lay a low marshy grassland where horses grazed in silhouette against a sunset sky. Here and there quiet pools reflected clouds of apricot gold. "It's like *White Mane!*" exclaimed Eve. It was. It could have been a scene from that beautiful semidocumentary filmed in the Camargue region of France. As a family, we had loved *White Mane* so much we'd seen it three times.

Above Trois-Rivières, the St. Lawrence is unaffected by the tide. Therefore these marshy flats were not salt like those of the Camargue. But they looked salt, and they reminded me of an *habitant* legend, "The Haycocks of Le Très Fort."

Generations ago along the south shore of the St. Lawrence, certain villagers had raised salt hay in a communal riverside field. But a certain giant, *Le Très Fort* (the Very Strong One), would always appear and make off with the crop. Eventually they gave up their thankless tending of that particular field and left it to the giant. All of them gave up, that is, except a poor widow and her daughter. Again, the two mowed their portion, turned it in the afternoon sun, raked it into cocks. Again *Le Très Fort* appeared. After pleading with him to leave their small harvest, the widow and her daughter returned home and prayed. Next morning the giant's haycocks had turned to stone while theirs remained sweet and fragrant.

Camargue views continued the next day along the bank and over to long low islands offshore. It was as hot as the south of France, too.

"From here on it's got to be good," said Jim on our next-to-last day. "We've had all our trouble: heat, rain, poison ivy—,"

"Garbage—"

"Other acky smells—"

"Gravel—"

"Sore feet—"

"Sore knees, sleepless nights—"

How naive can you get? There was no law against repeats. Came now road work and pipe laying in quick succession, to the accompaniment of coarse, sharp gravel. Even the children and I groaned. For although we weren't really footsore, our shoes were the ones we'd started in, and four hundred miles plus had honed their soles to a fine, sensitive thinness.

In perverse mood, Jim threw his walking stick into the ditch. "That's the end of that dumb *baton*," he grouched. The children stifled their giggles. I thought of Coleridge's broom-handle walking stick. We were parting company with a great tradition. So, each occupied with his own gloomy thoughts, we trudged on.

Soon, faint horrid whiffs began to float our way from what looked like a large factory a mile or so distant. The closer we got, the worse the air became. People driving past rolled up their windows and pushed down on their accelerators. We tied wet hankerchiefs over our faces and speeded up as best we could. It was a paint factory.

Eve, who had claustrophobic tendencies, protested from behind her handkerchief, "I can't stand it. I've got to take it off."

"Remember what we said on the Richelieu drawbridge," I said pitilessly from behind mine. "Be a good sport."

Thursday night the lights of Montreal were visible just upstream and across the river from Varennes. After dinner, while Dave and Eve shared with two French youngsters some of the sparklers bought in Quebec, Jim and I eyed the city, so near and yet so far.

Later as the four of us took turns in the shower, there was discussion—first this threesome, then that, then the other. The adversities of the last few days and the prospect of a worse day to come had filled us, one and all, with disgust.

According to my large-scale map, we were just across the river from the northeast section of Montreal.

"We've really walked to Montreal," someone said. "Why don't we just take the bus to town tomorrow?"

No, that would be cheating.

"But if we were to hire someone to take us across the river in a boat. . . ."

("Somebody else can have the shower now.")

The boat idea sounded more interesting. We could forgive ourselves for not swimming over.

"We knew it was going to be tough. On the Richelieu drawbridge we agreed to be good sports."

"Yes. But it didn't have to be all this tough."

"Binkie, look at the bottom of my left foot and tell me what you see. . . . We might spend half the day trying to find someone with a boat to take us across and then maybe miss our train."

"Here, hold it up to the light." Why had I not examined my spouse's extremities miles ago? No wonder he'd griped! On the ball of his foot he had a plantar wart of awesome size, a museum piece.

("Next in the shower.")

When I described it to him, he swelled with pride. "Four hundred and two miles on a plantar wart! That must be some kind of record."

I was glad I had brought a razor blade. "Now, hold still and I'll do a little surgery." It was not a definitive treatment, but it would certainly make walking less painful.

As I went into the shower I heard him say, "Children, your father is a great stoic. He has walked 402 miles on a plantar wart."

"Are we going to walk the rest of the way?"

"What do you vote?"

"Well, O.K., we came this far—"

"What time do we have to get up?"

"Five o'clock."

Groans. "Dit-dit-dit-dit . . . dit . . . dit-dah-dit-dit . . . dit-dah-dit-dit." On the two "l's" Eve chimed in. She had learned to spell "hell" in Morse code.

"We don't need that long," argued Dave, "to do thirteen and a half miles by three o'clock."

"We have to allow for contingencies. We can't afford to miss our train."

"We'll never get breakfast that early."

"Mama has some bananas and a can of tomato juice."

"Well, O.K., but only if you promise me more privileges this winter."

"Me too."

"Remember the drawbridge," I said, coming out of the shower. "Good sports don't drive bargains."

HAT OVERBOARD

VARENNES still slept. For once we departed a town before its church bells had begun to ring. It was not yet six; the sun was not up. Under a blanket of mist, the air was chill. What few motorists there were drove with their headlights on.

Each stomach containing a banana and half a glass of tomato juice, we filed silently out of Varennes.

"How far to the next town, Binkie?" Jim asked.

"Six miles to Boucherville."

"That's for us. We'll be able to get a real breakfast there."

When we'd walked a mile or so, the sun rose like the Japanese flag—a red ball in an expanse of white. The river and the islands were swathed in mist, and Montreal was invisible.

People who crave hamburgers and milkshakes for breakfast should have them. Boucherville did not object.

From there on, factories made a dreary landscape and commuter traffic kept us noisy company, but we remembered the drawbridge.

Presently at Longueuil, just opposite Montreal, another bridge emerged impressively out of the mist—the more-than-two-mile Jacques Cartier Bridge.

Well before noon we were on its pedestrian path, walking toward the glamorous Montreal skyline; pausing now and then to look over the side onto the decks of freighters, liners, lumber schooners, tugboats. And catching our breath at the bedspring bouncing we got whenever a heavy truck passed. The bridge trembled but it didn't collapse. Nor had it collapsed during construction, nor during any cold snap. Nor even when engineers had raised it several feet to meet St. Lawrence Seaway specifications. Hail, Jacques Cartier Bridge!

In the center of the center span there had to be a significant happening, for that point surely represented the city limits of Montreal. The "dumb trip," as David had called it, was over. We had come safely through twenty-seven days of walking and six days of layover. "I've kept watch and wart over you," said the *père de famille*.

We hadn't walked around the world as our young friends at

Disraeli had wanted to believe we were doing. Nor walked across Canada. Nor even scratched the surface of that enormous, twice-as-big-as-Texas place, Quebec Province. But we knew we'd been somewhere, and despite all our troubles and gripes, we'd had a good time.

Yes, something special was called for at the center of the bridge.

Overcome by the drama of the moment, Jim indulged in that supreme gesture of liberation which has so long been the exclusive privilege of the male sex: he flung his hat into the air. And into the water.

The rest of us gasped. He had threatened to do it but we hadn't believed he really would. It was a costly imported tweed. Our puritan blood leapt in our veins.

"That's crazy," said Dave. "At least you had some reason for getting rid of all those shoes if they didn't fit you. And someone else will get the good of them. But—"

"Well," Eve reminded her brother, "you threw away two hats yourself!"

"I left them where somebody could find them. Besides, they didn't cost twenty dollars."

"I'd have done it if the hat had cost forty dollars."

"It's immoral," said Eve indignantly.

"I've never owned a twenty-dollar hat," I said self-righteously.

"And none of you" said Jim, "has ever walked 425 miles on a plantar wart."

"If you can throw away a twenty-dollar hat," said Dave with the elusive logic of a sixteen year old, "I can have more privileges this winter."

"Me too."

"I can stay up till ten-thirty."

"Me too."

"We'll see." They were astonished.

The Scotch tweed hat was an excellent floater. Jauntily, some 120 feet below us, it started on its thousand-mile journey to the sea, on the breast of the continent's fourth longest river. Starting about noon on August 28 from Montreal that *chapeau de tweed* must have reached the Atlantic soon after our arrival home in Cedar Rapids.

From there, who knows? Perhaps the Gulf Stream carried it home to Scotland. If so, what it found there I know not.

What we found when we got home was a fat bunch of mail, including a copy of the Sherbrooke *Daily Record* in which appeared a group picture of "Iowa French Teacher and Family" and the reporter's interview with us.

We rocked with laughter when we noticed an adjacent advertisement from a Sherbrooke chiropodist: "Learn More About Feet."

PART IV
Southern Crossing

KNAVE AND HERO IN ONE

"IZARRA," said the waiter, setting the drink before us. "It's the Basque word for 'the stars.' "

It seemed to sum up for us in advance all the poetry and fire of the proud people in whose land we were going to start our fourth long walking trip.

A liqueur made from the gentian bulb, and a specialty of the Basque country, Izarra comes in two colors. Eve and I thought we liked the green a bit better than the yellow.

"It's just the color that beguiles you," Jim remarked. "There's no difference in flavor."

Though Eve, just out of high school, was with us, David was now on his own, working in Alaska for the U.S. Forest Service. This summer we three were setting out to walk the French Pyrenees, from Atlantic to Mediterranean. Mountainous all the way, it would be the toughest thing we'd tackled.

If St-Jean-de-Luz, our starting point, was any indication, it would pale the earlier trips in interest. For, leaving aside its playground-of-the-rich aspects, this port on the Bay of Biscay is real, alive, and exciting. Fortunately the season had not yet begun. Not only were the promenades and casinos deserted and the rental gondolas bobbing idly on the water without occupants, but room rates were deliriously reasonable.

"I hope they aren't losing too much on us," Jim worried as he surveyed the dining room, empty except for us. "I hate to see an empty hotel."

The port itself, the mouth of the Nivelle River, was a busy place with tuna boats coming and going. Basque fishermen, lithe and rather small, stepped nimbly about the decks in rope-soled espadrilles. It was in their blood to sail the sea: some nine centuries earlier their ancestors were putting out in small boats to harpoon the whale whenever one was sighted from the lookout tower.

Basque fishermen were going from St-Jean to the Grand Banks off Newfoundland before Columbus discovered America. When, in 1713, the Treaty of Utrecht had greatly restricted the right of these early Luziens to fish on the Grand Banks, they had turned—what could be more natural?—to piracy.

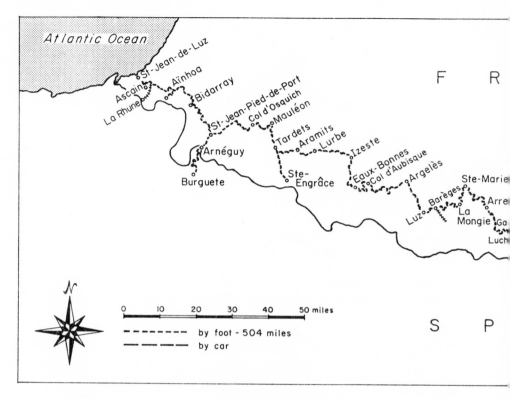

"Look," I said, as on a prowl we passed some sort of public building, "they've even inscribed famous French pirates' names on that building, the way we put Shakespeare, Goethe, and Milton on our libraries."

I was crestfallen to discover that this wasn't Jean Lafitte (one "f") the pirate, at all, but Jacques Laffitte (two "f's"), a staid French financier born in the region. But there definitely were Basque pirates in the seventeenth and eighteenth centuries.

Flapping in a brisk Atlantic breeze was the Basque flag, its three colors—red, green, and white—representing the three French Basque provinces (Labourd, Basse-Navarre, and Soule) and its four quarters representing the four Spanish Basque provinces (Viscaya, Guipúzcoa, Álava, and Navarra). The three plus four added up to seven, and *Zaspiak bat*, the motto of all the Basques, added up in translation to "Seven as One."

Berets were in evidence, as well as wide red sashes.

Across the Nivelle, neighboring Ciboure (or, as the Basques call it, Zubiburu) was devoid of luxury hotels, beach clubs, promenades, and casinos. Zubiburu gave us our first glimpse of the *cascarots*. They looked like gypsies and dressed like them. Actually they are

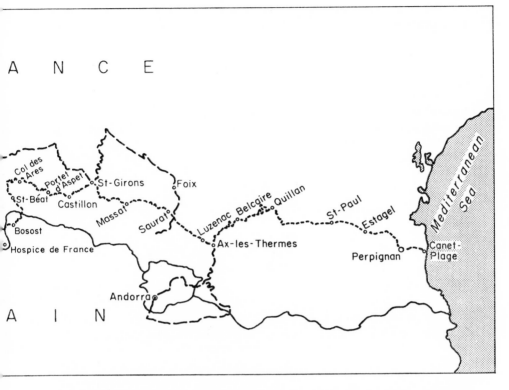

descendants of gypsies who, driven out of Spain in the sixteenth century, intermarried with the *cagots*, members of the medieval French leper caste. At Zubiburu the *cascarots* ply their calling as fishermen, alongside the Basques, and their women carry the catch to market.

In Zubiburu's church, which was graced by a Madonna clad Spanish style in gold-embroidered black, a miniature ship hung from the ceiling. No doubt it spoke of gratitude to the Virgin for her having saved some tuna boat, some whaler, perhaps even some privateer, from marine disaster.

In the church we picked up mimeographed words to a Basque hymn:

Apezaren eskaintza onhar zazu Jauna
Hilek dezaten goza, zure zoriona.
Zato, Zato ene Jesus maitea,
Zu zare zu ene ontasuna.
Oi zer dohain ezin presatuzkoa.
Huna Jesus, ene zoriona.
Huna Jesus, huna Jesus!

What a strange language indeed was this Euskara! No wonder it baffled linguists. Different scholars have claimed to see in it a relationship to Finnish, Berber, Eskimo, Sanskrit. Still another theory holds that it's the tongue of the "lost continent" of the Atlantic. The Basques themselves believe, or used to, that they speak the language of Eden.

To us it appeared to have some similarity to Japanese. As far as stature was concerned, the Basques were not unlike the Japanese, but the resemblance ended there. Besides, how could they have gotten all the way to the Iberian Peninsula? We settled for having our Izarra waiter translate the hymn:

> Receive, O Lord, the offering of the priest
> That our dead may enjoy your blessing.
> Come, O come, Jesus my beloved,
> You are my treasure.
> What a priceless gift.
> Behold Jesus, my happiness.
> Behold Jesus, behold Jesus!

The Izarra had topped off an excellent dinner. A while later the three of us stood on an upstairs balcony listening to tender cooing of pigeons in someone's dovecote and inhaling across tile roofs the perfume of a million subtropical blossoms. We watched the lights come on along the St-Jean waterfront. Silhouetted against the Spanish sky was La Rhune, the last considerable peak, the westernmost outpost of the Pyrenees range, and the legendary abode of witches.

While we listened and smelled and looked, gradually all the sky was pricked with a multitude of fiery Basque diamonds—the *izarra*.

The critic Lemaître said of novelist Pierre Loti that his art was so simple it was impossible to discover "how it was done." Lyrically but authentically Loti depicted in *Ramuntcho* (1897) Basque life as it was in the late nineteenth century. His hero, Ramuntcho, has become the Basque prototype for all time.

Our first night out from St-Jean-de-Luz was to be spent in the Ascain hotel where Loti lived while writing the novel.

It was only five miles up the Nivelle valley to Ascain, a nice short hike for our first day. It was good to be on the road again, putting one foot in front of the other and feeling the fine self-reliance of knapsack on shoulders.

The knapsacks, however, stayed at the hotel in Ascain, when, after lunch there, we walked on up beyond, to the Col St-Ignace. Traveling light that way, we strode as though wearing seven-league boots.

The word *col,* the concept *col,* was to be with us night and day in the weeks to come. We were heading eastward, generally parallel to that great backbone, the Pyrenees, and we'd have to climb up and over its many spurs or vertebrae. *Cols* are east-west passes over the vertebrae, as distinct from *ports,* north-south passes over the main backbone.

At the summit of this particular *col* was the lower end of a funicular railway running to the top of La Rhune, that westernmost mountain peak we'd seen from our balcony. We caught the last scheduled departure of the small, open-sided train.

Here and there on the steep slopes, wiry fellows in berets stood hip deep in ferns, swinging their scythes through them with rhythmic ease. When this *fougère* had dried, they would haul it down to their stables to serve as litter. Big fat ewes, most of them yet unshorn, looked up in blank amaze as the train passed. Witches, we saw none.

When we stepped off the funicular at the upper terminal, the ocean was spread out to the west, some three thousand feet below us. The frontier runs right through La Rhune's summit, and accordion music floated over from the cafe shop in Spain as irresistible as the lyre of Orpheus. Suddenly we were seized by the Basque passion for turning to advantage the French-Spanish border.

Before 1669, these proud and independent people had enjoyed privileges of the frontier not enjoyed elsewhere in the Pyrenees. Like the fishermen-turned-pirates, nonfishing Basques whose border privileges were revoked became *hors-la-loi* ("outlaws"). They turned to smuggling which they developed into an art. Over mountain pass and across turbulent stream, the sturdy Basque carried his contraband goods on his back. The blacker, the stormier the night, the better. The modern Basque, it was said, would even disassemble whole automobiles and carry them across in installments, to reassemble and sell them on the other side! It was a sporting contest played with equal verve by the customs guards—a contest that still goes on today.

"I want to get some espadrilles," I announced. "Hilaire Belloc says rope soles are best for walking in the Pyrenees."

"You're mad," said Jim. "Stick to your Marine Corps boots."

"But I'd love a pair to relax in when we get to our destination every night."

"You can get them in France. I saw them in St-Jean."

"But I want Spanish espadrilles."

"You'll just be adding weight to your load. I for one am going to buy a *boina* ('Basque beret') and some strong Spanish cigarettes and some cheap Pernod. Maybe even a *bota* ('wine skin')."

"I want a Spanish shawl," said Eve. "And let's get some Spanish chocolate."

Amid a bedlam of music, voices, and clatter of glasses and bottles, we were able to buy everything except the *bota,* the right *boina,* and the right Spanish shawl. It was, of course, quite aboveboard. There was nothing illegal about riding a funicular to the frontier, buying Spanish espadrilles, cigarettes, Pernod, and chocolate, and returning with them to France. But this was a corner of the world celebrated for its smugglers. We had an irrational, exhilarating, daring feeling. And prices were a bit cheaper in Spain.

At dusk in Ascain, the village *fronton* rang with the cries of pelota players and with the sharp crack of the ball against wooden paddles and stone backstop. The spirited contest of the *fronton,* a court consisting of front wall, sidewall, and back wall, was to be a constant of our two weeks in the land of the Basques. At Ascain, the village priest was playing, bounding about very agilely despite his skirts, and with him three young men. Loti's Ramuntcho was a master at this super handball game (in the Basque tongue, *jai-alai, or* "merry festival"), always scoring the points that won for his village.

Ramuntcho led a double life. Besides being a winning pelota player, he was a wily outwitter of the customs guards. Like him, would one of these young men of Ascain, when full darkness fell, turn smuggler and take off for Spain with some forbidden burden on his back? Secretly I hoped so.

Just when Loti's busy Basque knave found time for sleeping was not clear, but we could not do without ours. We turned in.

SATAN, SANTIAGO, AND SHAKESPEARE

"HOLD her hands!" cried Jim to Eve. We were about to meet another team of blond oxen hauling a load of hay. My mate felt I'd already taken enough hay pictures to last a lifetime. Deferring to him I missed my only chance at a shot of oxen wearing bright red pom-poms bobbing over their eyes to keep the flies away. But later in the day when Jim wasn't looking, I snapped a father and son erecting a towering haystack. Son brought forkful after forkful which father, on top, tamped down each time with an efficient knee.

Children were everywhere for it was Thursday, a school holiday in France. Birds were warbling. Cherries were ripe, both red ones and black.

The farmhouses, facing east because the rain generally comes from the west, were spick and span, most of them having been freshly whitewashed for the Fête-de-St-Jean. Against the green of the fields, their red tile roofs sang with color.

An old custom that modern Basques retain is that of primogeniture. Farms pass intact from father (*etchako jaun*) to firstborn or to heir-designate, without being divided and redivided into smaller and smaller parcels. We were seeing several generations working together on the land and living under one roof in the *etcheonda* ("stem house"). Under that same roof, to one side, were the animals—sleeping on beds of fern while the people slept on mattresses stuffed with wool.

As usual, our knapsacks contained food, and the Basques, like the northern French, were neither annoyed nor surprised to have us dig out bread and salami or cheese to eat with the drinks we ordered in their cafes.

Sare, where we made one such stop, was Ramuntcho's village, though in the book it goes by its Basque name "Etchezar."

Grouped about the double heart of the village—the church and the pelota *fronton*—were the simple sturdy houses of *torchis*, an adobelike mixture of clay and straw, whitewashed a brilliant white. The heavy exposed timbers were painted a warm russet. (In another village, in a ground-floor wine "cave," one beam was nearly two feet thick each way.)

Speculation about the age of these Basque houses was seldom necessary, for whether in the village or out in the country, there was almost always a construction date over the door, usually accompanied by the family name, often by a motto, and possibly the circumstances of building. Some dated back to before the time when the Pyrenean provinces were added to the French kingdom.

Youthful pelota players at Sare were using, instead of the wooden paddle or the leather "palm," the wicker *chistera*. But all three versions, plus sometimes the bare hand, are authentic in jai-alai, and before our walk was over we'd see them all.

Though Loti had chosen Sare as the setting of *Ramuntcho*, Aïnhoa, our second night's stop, was perhaps the "perfect" Basque village. The *fronton* was next to the church, which in earlier times was fortified. Just back of the village, a Way of the Cross led up a hill to a chapel. In the churchyard were curious discoid gravestones dating from the sixteenth and seventeenth centuries, many displaying the Basque cross, a rounded form of the swastika. Did this lend fuel to the theory that the Basques had come from India, where the swastika is a very ancient symbol? Another question mark over this strange people!

Before dinner I installed myself on the balcony of one of our two bedrooms to rub our shoes with GI dubbing to make them water resistant. Below me, a man wearing beret and red sash was sawing wood, and nearby another was picking lettuce. Children and women and dogs of Aïnhoa were making a happy commotion, and the smell of pimento-seasoned chicken *à la basquaise* floated up from the kitchen. Moments of peace and expectancy!

In Basse-Navarre, second of the French Basque provinces, farm and forest alternated, wild mint grew by the roadside, and we heard the cuckoo sing. Geese in small pens, where three times daily they were force-fed through tubes to create *foie gras* for gourmet palates, appalled us.

"I'll never eat *foie gras* again," declared Eve. It was easy for us to agree. Costly status foods were not our dish anyway.

At Bidarray a donkey-back bridge, the Pont d'Enfer, or Bridge of Hell, had its story.

"The Devil," I informed my less literate companions, "threw himself from this bridge because he couldn't learn the Basque language, and my sympathies are all with the poor devil. Just look at those words!"

Nearby was a poster announcing some sort of public merry-making.

ALTZAIN
UZTAILAREN 5ian
4 orenetan
ALTZAIARRAK
eta
ALTAZUKUTARRAK
zouin hobe iokietan?
Soka—Thiratze—Jaouzkan—Lasterkakan—Khantan
Pelotakan—Asto—Koursa, eta beste

8 Orenen	Indarkatik landa
Altian	Indarhartze
	Mahanian

Jin Altzaiat, Arratsalde Goxo Baten Igaitera

Said Eve: "If Basque was really the language of the Garden of Eden, the Devil must have known how to speak it, to tempt Eve." She had a delightful way of pricking myths.

"When I get my *boina*," Jim affirmed, "I expect to be able to read things like this at a glance." The rushing Nive River, where *le Diable* had met his aqueous end, flowed on, unimpressed by such vain talk.

The faucets at Bidarray were marked *eau non potable*—the sole instance of unsafe water on our whole Pyrenean trip. Could it have anything to do with Satan's having chosen this spot for his watery suicide?

Unforeseen and unsettling the next day, as we followed the Petit Nive upstream, was the postshower coming out of slugs. Not mustard colored slugs, like those we'd met and more or less conquered in northern France, but coal black slugs. Of all the gruesome things in the natural world, these were surely the ugliest, the most disgusting. It definitely is difficult to love some forms of life! But pshaw, the sun came out and they went wherever slugs go.

Ancient walls girdle much of St-Jean-Pied-de-Port, and riverside houses bathe their feet in the water. An ancient citadel crowns its hill.

The "port" of St-Jean's title is Roncevaux Pass, which leads across into Spain. Through this pass Charlemagne was bringing his troops in 778 after a campaign against the Saracens in Spain, and here Roland (later to be immortalized in *The Song of Roland)* died along with others of the rear guard when the Basques, hidden in the mountain heights above, tumbled boulders and huge uprooted trees upon them.

Our pause at St-Jean was brief, for the plan was to get to Arnéguy, at the Spanish frontier, that night.

Steep though the slopes were, they were cultivated. In the late afternoon light, teams of oxen were drawing the plow. Seemingly they knew exactly what master or mistress wanted, though the Basque syllables didn't sound as though they could possibly make sense.

Here and there over doorways were bits of greenery arranged in the shape of a cross, in remembrance of the fact that this had been one of the popular routes over to Santiago de Compostela. In the Middle Ages, hordes of gray-clad pilgrims had trod this route, each carrying a cross of leafy branches to be deposited at the summit of the pass before proceeding to the holy shrine near Pontevedra.

"It must have looked like Birnam Wood coming to Dunsinane," said Jim. All agreed we'd like to have seen those picturesquely, pleasantly mad devotees of Santiago.

Later in the climb, with no thought of mimicking either *Macbeth* or the medieval pilgrims, Eve and I picked big stalks of fern to fight off clouds of cattle flies that attacked us. I even stuck ferns into my hatband to bob and wave the flies away.

"Binkie," said my ever-candid husband, "you look silly."

"So did Birnam Wood, sir, but Malcolm won the battle."

JUERGA BY CHANCE

AFTER about seventeen miles, all uphill, it was good to shed our knapsacks at Arnéguy. Part of the village, including the little hotel, was in France, the rest in Spain. As we ate our French Basque dinner we could watch frontier guards across the river, pacing up and down in Spain.

"My grandfather Clément," said Madame to us that evening, "used to live in that house just across the road there." She had found time to come and visit with us as we sat at a wee iron table squeezed in between the hotel and the road. For the moment, the wedding party in the dining room were apparently all served and happy, and no one was waiting to buy anything at the hole-in-wall bakery-grocery store she operated in a corner of the ground floor.

"The hotel, Clémentía, is named for our family," she went on in French. "Well, Grandfather Clément took it into his head one day to go to the United States. He borrowed the money to pay his passage, and he left a wife and nine children behind. He thought he'd make a fortune and send for them. Instead, three months later, without any warning, here he was back again. He had done all right. He just didn't like it over there. My grandmother was working in the field and someone said, 'Hey, look who's there—Clément!' He just appeared, coming up the road. That was his house right over there." The evening light on its whitewashed walls and the line of clean bright clothes hanging in the yard gave it all a storybook look.

But Clément's story wasn't typical. Thanks to primogeniture and to the Basque dislike of forced military service, the Western Hemisphere receives a steady stream of Basque immigrants (nearly a thousand a year): those who don't inherit the land and house and those who don't want to serve in the army. Lots of these *American-oaks,* Madame assured us, after making their fortune at sheepherding in North or South America, send for the family to join them. "But not Grandfather Clément—he just didn't like it."

This pleasant little woman was probably washing wedding banquet dishes long after we were in bed, but on the dot of seven, as arranged, she and a young helper appeared at Eve's and my door with a heavy oak table which they'd carried from downstairs. As usual in France, we were to breakfast upstairs, and she'd decided we needed a larger table. The one they lugged up must have weighed a hundred pounds.

When a little later we set off up the pass, I was carrying one of her homemade Basque cakes, still warm, which she wanted us to have *"pour manger plus tard"* ("to eat later").

In a matter of minutes we'd shown our passport four times, to two batches of French officials and two of Spanish. We were now in the Provincia de Navarra. Wooden balconies had been replaced by balconies of iron grille work. Generalissimo Franco's stern face looked at us from the wall of the guardhouse, and a sign proclaimed fanatically: *Todo por la Patria*.

Yet was it all that different?

Valcarlos, the first village up the gorge, could have been a village in Basque France. Boys were playing pelota at a *fronton,* one wall of which was a wall of the church. It was Sunday, and sounds of mass coming from the open door mingled with the cries of the young *pelotaris.* The faces were much the same; the bodies had that same wiry resilience; the language, as nearly as we could tell, was the same.

The real proof, though it was not visible, was the Basque blood. Frequency of CDe chromosomes is very high among the Basques, whether French or Spanish, while their cDE rate is the lowest in Europe. They're unusually high in O-type blood, low in the relatively common type B, and, of all peoples tested, highest in the Rh negative factor.

We knew nothing about our chromosomes, but we did know we were all Rh positive and that none of us was an O. Whatever their origin, in blood we had little or nothing in common with the Basques.

"But it's nice to know there are lots of O's among them," reflected Jim, with characterisic emphasis on the cheery side of things. "In case we should suddenly need transfusions. O blood can be given to anyone—even to us rare AB's."

The only common A in the family, I was constantly taunted in a very undemocratic way by the others, all AB's. "Someday it'll be proven that A is just as good as AB," I said, without believing it.

Of all the dim dark cafes we'd patronized—north, south, east or west—none had been quite so murky as that in which we consumed our delicious fruity *gâteau basque.*

The farther up the pass we climbed, the more the forest sounded like the birdhouse at a zoo. Chirps, trills, warbles, obbligatos, squawks, hoots, whistles, yawps, descants, and twitters: all were there, and woven in with them the sound of running water somewhere, and the distant musical tinkle of *clarines* around the necks of Spanish sheep.

Los Animales no Saben lo que Hacen. Tu Si. Un Carro Solo Es un Peligro. No Abandiones sus Riendas. Among us we managed to translate it: "Animals don't know what they're doing. You do. A cart without a driver is a danger. Don't let go of the reins."

On the near side of the summit was a platform in a tall tree. This was where, in October, the local Basque hunters would stretch a great net across the gap in the mountains, would station beaters in trees to utter guttural cries, wave white flags, and launch wooden sparrowhawks into the great southbound flights of wild doves. The thought of the pitiful, wholesale panic of hundreds, even thousands, of *palomas* entangled in the net saddened us.

A favorite Basque song runs, "White dove, where are you going? The mountains of Spain are covered with snow. You have for tonight a refuge in our house." I hoped the refuge mentioned wasn't a cooking pot.

A cold wind greeted us at the top of the pass, and the day was too hazy for us to see Brittany, some 370 miles to the north, as is sometimes possible. By the time we reached Roncevaux, about a mile down the other side, we were in the mood for something warming. The village was unpromising.

In the days when Santiago de Compostela had rivalled Rome as a shrine, Roncevaux had served some thirty thousand pilgrim meals a year, but now, alack, we saw only a huge church, a large convent, a small chapel to Santiago, ancient buildings with modern corrugated-iron roofs, priests strolling about. Most unpromising.

But wait! Song and sounds of stomping were coming from a small building inconspicuously marked *Restaurante*.

Seven glasses stood empty on one of the tables. What potent elixir they had contained could only be surmised from the way seven Basques were dancing, singing, clapping, stomping their heels on the bare wood floor, drumming on chair seats, and generally raising a fine flamenco uproar.

They were much too engrossed in their *juerga* to notice three knapsacked strangers slip furtively to a table in a far corner. From there we watched and listened spellbound, while sipping the blackest, thickest coffee this side of Arabia.

Focus of interest was a pair of swarthy fellows of typical slight build with typical narrow, rather triangular faces. The one in the dark red shirt had pulled his soft straw hat down rakishly over one eye. His hatless, wavy-haired stooge, a perfect comedian type, kept flicking the light switch off and on, with appropriate wisecracks. Some of his remarks seemed to refer to the only other spectators in the room, a pretty blonde and her escort, both Spanish but obviously not of the village.

A short blond fellow, wearing his sweater tied around his waist by its sleeves, seemed to feel the rhythm of the songs especially in his elbows. While the rest of his body remained as motionless and tense as that of a stalking cat, he literally danced with his elbows.

Another blond, whose tall stature and broad shoulders as well as his fair hair indicated some admixture to the Basque blood, started up a new song from time to time. We couldn't be sure, but he seemed to be improvising at least the words. If so, he was right in the Basque tradition.

No guitar. No musical instrument at all. Just seven resonant voice boxes, the palms of fourteen hands, the fourteen leather heels, the floor, the chair seats, the table top.

When the lights-off-lights-on routine began to pall, another character came unexpectedly to the fore. Though he looked like a businessman—gray-haired, conservatively dressed, smoking a cigar—he pulled a knife from his pocket, flipped it open in a flash, and with its long shiny blade he threatened the one with the rakish straw hat.

We caught our breath, wishing we weren't so far from the door. And then we relaxed. For it was all in the spirit of clowning! The singing went on, as well as the dancing, the laughter, the grimaces, the stomping heels, the clapping hands, the snapping fingers, the dancing elbows. Thus our introduction to a Spanish trait: the "mock mayhem syndrome."

THE MAN WHO COULDN'T STOP TALKING

A STEALTHY man with a slingshot lurked near the Santiago chapel as we left Roncevaux. Young people were dancing on a flat grassy spot. Farther on, under beech trees that lined the road, dozens of families were gathering tiny wild strawberries. All of which underlined the fact it was Saturday.

The hotel at Burguete was booked full, but Madame at Arnéguy had somehow found time to arrange quarters for us in a private home.

It was a big house with wide stairway and halls, great oaken beams, a huge fireplace with brass vessels on the mantel above it, cows and chickens in part of the downstairs, and a pervading chill and dampness throughout. Our two rooms were spotless.

Fainting with hunger in this land of nine o'clock *comida* ("dinner"), we walked around the village, watched pelota at an indoor *fronton,* then sat awhile in the church. Here, women and girls were twining flowers around, on, and above the altar, climbing on it as nonchalantly as though it had been the platform of a school auditorium. What the flowers on the altar were all about, we learned next morning.

Singing and the sound of guitars woke me at 6:20. Bounding to the window and throwing open the shutters, I beheld in the street below some twenty or twenty-five people, several of them holding umbrellas, for it was raining. They were serenading beneath the window of a house across from us. Finally they disappeared down the street, and a little later the sound of rockets shattered the Sunday silence.

Impatient to get outdoors, to get breakfast at the hotel over with, and to get into the thick of whatever was happening, I nagged, coaxed, begged Jim and Eve to hurry. Under no circumstances must we miss a moment of the doings!

Once out in the thick of it, we only had to wait about four hours. Ah, Spain! Ah, spirit of *mañana!*

A boy sauntered down the street with an armload of rockets. Another was sweeping the plaza with a twig broom, in adagio tempo. Across the entrance to the church had been strung garlands of greenery and a banner: *Burguete Te Felicita, las Almas Te Esperan* ("Burguete congratulates you, souls await you").

People stood around. Endlessly patient, they stood and stood and stood. The rain had stopped and the sun was out.

It hadn't been hard to deduce from the sign that they were welcoming some ecclesiastical personage. From a gentleman whose smattering of French came to the aid of our smattering of Spanish, we learned that a young man of Burguete who'd been away studying for the priesthood was returning, now an ordained priest, to say his first mass in his home village. In addition, it was the Fiesta San Pietro, a favorite saint day.

No hurry! Everyone was quite content just standing around. Women stood around in their black lace mantillas. Men stood around bareheaded or bereted. Altar boys stood at the church door, in red and white satin. We stood first on one foot, then on the other.

It was after 1:30 when a priest appeared from somewhere, carrying an armload of rich red and gold vestments into the church.

Suddenly recorded music blared forth. Our friend told us in his mixture of French and Spanish that the Basque flute we were hearing has only three holes, and by gesture he indicated that it is blown from the end rather than from the side. It was called the *tchirula.* The drum (he beat an imaginary tattoo on an imaginary drum) was appropriately called the *ttun-ttun.*

Presently there came into sight, progressing on foot up the crowded street, a group of priests. Front and center was a tall, dark, and handsome young fellow, bowing and waving to his friends. Rockets went off. There was no shouting, only a low murmur of excitement and approval. In went the priests; after them, the crowd; after them, the Youngs. The service was in Latin and Spanish, and the sermon made frequent reference to the new young priest and to his mother and sister, who were present.

Hot potato salad led off the fiesta luncheon at the hotel. Hungry though we were and good though the food, we could hardly take our eyes off the big horseshoe table where were gathered, after mass, the young priest, his proud and happy mother and sister, his ecclesiastical colleagues, and relatives and friends from babes to hoary patriarchs.

As the rough, chilled red wine flowed, the babble crescendoed. It was like a fully animated gallery of Velasquez, Murillo, and El Greco portraits.

"Souls await you," the banner had said. We didn't know anything about that, but it was evident the young priest was persona grata in his home town.

"Good morning, good morning," Jim greeted me. "Let's get going, let's get going."

"*Si Señor*," said I, feeling very Spanish, "but why the double talk?"

"Haven't you noticed? Haven't you noticed? It's the clocks that have done this to me. It's the clocks that have done this to me."

It was so. The clocks in our *casa* and the bells of Burguete's church did repeat everything they struck. It was rather cryptic. What was the true hour, the first strike or the second? Perhaps only an American would ask.

Nearly one hundred kilometers (sixty-two miles) in five days, plus the relaxing day at Burguete, had put us in excellent trim—a good thing, for we were going to trek not only over Roland's pass again to Arnéguy, but on beyond to St-Jean-Pied-de-Port.

A heavy fog bathed the pass, and we walked in our blast jackets for warmth and dryness. Beyond the summit but still in Spain, a gang of roadworkers were moving at a very Monday morning pace. Bits of rock they'd chipped were gathered in round baskets and carried, at funeral gait, to where they were needed.

Seeing my camera, these Spanish fellows asked me to take their picture and immediately posed with one of them seemingly about to land his sledgehammer on the head of a fellow worker. Like our friends at the *juerga,* they found make-believe violence hilarious.

Beside the next switchback, another of the gang was tending lunch for all. He had a nice bed of coals and in it seven or eight individual earthenware casseroles and one big one.

With utter insensitivity to human feelings, he explained to us how we might have saved four kilometers on a shortcut from Burguete.

Silently cursing him, his mysterious casseroles, and his after-the-fact shortcut, we continued our descent, found an inviting log and sat on it to eat our bread and good strong Spanish cheese.

Determined to spend our last pesetas before crossing the frontier, we canvassed Valcarlos for the right Spanish shawl, and, instead, bought only some Spanish playing cards from an old woman with a mustache. Four more passport showings and, presto, we were once more in France.

"My grandfather has left a foot in the Crimea," a young Basque in his twenties told us.

None of us could recall afterward how the conversation got started. All we knew was that we'd hauled into St-Jean-Pied-de-Port late, tired, and famished, that our hotel, having no dining room, had sent us down the street to eat, and that on the way this young man collared us to practice his English.

Growing weaker by the moment, Eve and I leaned against each other for support while he talked on.

"He was a fearsome sight, my grandfather, as he mounted his horse, with his beard and his one leg lacking its foot."

Jim swayed and a glassy look came over his eyes.

"My little sister, who has eleven years, saw you here Friday. She thought you, Monsieur, were a Boer."

It was getting chilly. Eve went back for our sweaters.

"It is pity you have not come in July. You could march toward Santiago for the name day. Our city was the unity place for three roads from the north. Here the pilgrims joined for the traveling on together. Santiago was at that epoch like Jerusalem. . . . You will take your dinner at the Hôtel Centrale? It is necessary to command some wine Irouléguy."

At the mention of wine Jim perked up, and the young man gathered fresh energy. "This is the Basque wine the most celebrated. One grows it very approximate to this city. It is extremely estimated."

Eve returned with the sweaters.

We praised his English for the third or fourth time and broke away as he assured us he was very "gladdy" to have met us.

We were gladdy to sit down at a terrace table and command not only the extremely estimated wine but the quickest possible dinner. It was after nine-thirty and even Spain had not tortured us thus.

A GREAT OAK

IT was good to be back in France. For one thing, speaking the language was more to our liking than using gestures.

For another, there was the custom of eating and drinking *en plein air*, about which there is something joyous and participatory. Even discounting the rather damp weather in Spain, it seemed to us that there'd been fewer sidewalk tables there, fewer eating terraces and balconies. Spanish architecture was definitely more introverted.

Here in St-Jean-Pied-de-Port, swallows zoomed almost within reaching distance as we breakfasted, and during the day's hike we restored ourselves more than once at an outdoor cafe.

From one, we could have reached out and handed a cool drink to the farmer who was driving his cattle through the village. He appeared to be calling each one by name. Narrow face, faded blue black beret on his head, hand-rolled cigarette hanging from the corner of his mouth, scythe over one shoulder, *aiguillon* ("goad of medlar wood") in the other hand, whetstone in horn sheath hanging from rope belt, espadrilles on his feet. Though he perhaps could not have named the President of France, he knew things that General de Gaulle would never know, about cattle, sheep, corn, and possibly contraband.

The afternoon was waning. For company as we started up a woodsy *col*, we had three schoolboys. Carrying briefcases and chattering first among themselves and then with us, they seemed very high spirited. The reason came out just before they turned off on the path to their village. This had been the last day of school.

The higher we got on the Col d'Osquich, the broader the views. What were those rows of brown dots down there? Beehives.

On we plodded. From one spot, four great flocks of sheep were visible at four widely scattered locations. What was that black speck that moved so fast? A sheep dog. Capably he headed off each beige speck that started to wander away from the flock. Still onward and upward we plodded.

At Col d'Osquich (elevation 1,650 feet, almost three times as high as Col St-Ignace) waited our first taste of the famous *confit basque* ("potted pork or poultry"—in this case duck). And our first night on a *col*.

Short of an actual mountain peak, there's no finer place to wake up than on a *col*. A cow, looking in our open window, gave us *bonjour*, and as we took off after breakfast gave us *bon voyage*.

At midday, in Ordiart, where several men were holding a lengthy conversation in the tongue that had baffled the Devil, the cafe woman had neither ice for our drinks nor an electric iron. She was attacking a mountain of linen with sadirons, but paused long enough to show us a picture of the local people dressed up for one of their old-time *pastorales*. These plays had *bons et mauvais* ("good guys and bad guys"). The *bons*, dressed in blue and headed by the bishop, always entered from the right side, and the *mauvais*, dressed in red, headed by the Devil, came in from the left.

"Eh bien," she sighed, "tout ça est passé." ("All that is gone.") And she quoted an old proverb. "Autre fois comme cela. Aujourd'hui comme ceci. Après, on ne sait comment." ("Yesterday that way. Today this way. Tomorrow, who knows.") She probably had no idea that the yesterday of *pastorales* reached clear back into the Middle Ages.

Her husband came in whistling. Like most Basques, he knew a good deal about California, Nevada, Oregon, Idaho, Wyoming, and South America. Every Basque seems to have some cousin, usually a sheepherder, across the ocean.

Ignatius Loyola and Francis Xavier, he told us proudly, were both *Eskualdunaks*, and that was how we learned what the Basques call themselves. Each Basque household, he further informed us, likes to have its three pigs. As Iowans, we were pleased to hear it.

"Must have been something special about that pop," I speculated when we got up to move on. "Usually my joints are a bit creaky after one of these stops."

"It's well known that iced drinks are bad for athletes," Jim replied. "You're not stiff because our drinks were tepid. As for me, I intend to go right on getting ice whenever I can."

The church at Libbarenx introduced us to an architectural feature peculiar to this third and easternmost French Basque province Soule: the "trinity" bell tower—three identical gabled towers topped by crosses and symbolizing, of course, the Holy Trinity.

Among the beautiful ripe-apricot-colored tile roofs we began to see tall roofs of hand-hewn slate with dormer windows. Above the door now, instead of greenery in the shape of cross, wreath, or spray, there appeared a small cross of wood or stone, into which were often twined fresh flowers.

Fireplaces—some of them used for cooking, with adjustable chain and hook for pots—were so big a person could stand erect in them and look up at the sky.

From the kitchen of such a house, at Menditte, I heard familiar syllables: *"Au galop, au galop, au galop!"* A grandmother was saying in French, to a cooing youngster, the same action verse that had enchanted me half a century before as I rode my mother's foot:

> This is the way the poor man goes:
> Step, by step, by step.
> This is the way the farmer goes:
> Trot, trot, trot, trot, trot.
> This is the way the rich man goes:
> *Au galop, au galop, au galop!*

No doubt my mother had heard the verse in French from her French grandmother, and had passed it on to me in English, keeping the last line in French. It gave me a strange thrill to hear it now, so far from home.

As we left Menditte, an enormous oak caught my eye. I'd read about Guernikako Arbola, the great oak at Guernica, Spain, which for centuries had symbolized the *fueros* or local liberties enjoyed by Basques, both French and Spanish.

Under Guernikako Arbola, monarchs had sworn to observe Basque rights. In a day when crown representatives had governed locally, these proud *Eskualdunaks* had insisted they would elect their own local officials, and that they would refuse military service except in the national defense and then only commanded by their own local officers. Under Guernikako Arbola, Basque laws had been made and Basque officials sworn in. The old oak had come to symbolize Basque unity, despite the fact that some Basques were French and some Spanish. *Zazpiak bat*—Seven as One.

I shuddered to think of Picasso's "Guernica" and what I'd read about the first modern bombing of a city, on April 26, 1937. It was a market day. First, machine guns; then bombs; and finally incendiary bombs. The waves of German planes came over the undefended town every twenty minutes from 4:30 in the afternoon until 7:45 that night, and when it was over, 1,654 had been killed and 889 wounded. Whether by deliberate forbearance, divine intervention, or mere chance, the sacred tree came through unscathed. As did also the Basque parliament building and the *fronton*. The heroic firemen of Guernica saved the church.

This Menditte oak looked large enough, strong enough, venerable enough to be the French counterpart of the Guernica tree.

INDEPENDENCE DAY
AND A RECKONING

WHILE Jim shopped for his beret at Tardets, Eve and I hung a wash on our balcony within sight and sound of the Saison. Fishermen were wading its wide gravelly shallows. Far off to the southern horizon, range after range receded in the purple haze of mountain distance. We'd be heading that way the next day.

In the morning, when Madame our hostess set our breakfast tray on the balcony table, she glanced out at the river where bright sun glinted on the riffles. "Uhaitz-Handi is our Basque name for the Saison," she said. "It means great torrent." It didn't seem very apt. The river was shallow and unimportant looking.

The day got hotter and the climb was plenty steep. Beautiful butterflies of all colors flashed against the green. Wild pinks grew in open places. Magpies made changing black and white patterns in the sky.

At a lonely roadside house displaying a battered cafe license, we roused the old woman from her siesta and asked for pop. With eyes roughly half open, she served us some lukewarm drinks, and I told myself it was really more healthful this way.

By now the river was far below us in a deep narrow gorge. A sign announced that this was a dangerous watercourse because hydroelectric operations might suddenly raise the water level without warning. That cool, inviting spot down there beside the modest stream would be the wrong place to be when someone opened the sluice gates up above. "Uhaitz-Handi," she'd said: "great torrent." It could be un-handi.

The deserted road became narrower and steeper yet. Mountainside farms continued, though. A bantam farmer, carrying what appeared to be his own weight in hay from stack to wagon in a kind of hod, asked where we were going. When we said Ste-Engrâce, he waxed eloquent. "Be sure," he said, "to notice the eyes of the daughter of the innkeeper." A tantalizing remark.

Though this was still France, the Spanish frontier was near. The road, the only one in the vicinity, would come to a dead end at Ste-Engrâce. But here was a large barracks, housing customs guards. How could there be enough traffic along this narrow, soon-to-end dirt track to keep more than a single guard busy?

We decided the score or more who bunked here must be really tough hombres, patrolling on foot a frontier that snakes among jagged peaks and glaciated cirques. It must be more than mere legend, this Basque smuggling thing. It must still go on.

A slight young man, not especially tough looking, was on duty and invited us to join him listening to a broadcast about the Tour de France. The racers in this French bicycle classic were now in Andorra. They were in even more vertical country than we. Just thinking about the grades they were negotiating made our legs ache and our egos shrink.

Beyond the customs station, a large dam backed the Uhaitz-Handi far into the gorge, forming a deep winding green lake with precipitous banks. Now we really saw what they meant about the water level rising without warning.

"It's probably good we couldn't buy firecrackers in Tardets," said Eve. "We might have started a flood with them."

"We ought to do something to celebrate the Fourth," I grumbled.

"Champagne," said the head of the family.

"Without ice?"

"There'll be ice."

Incredible but true: there was champagne and there was ice at the little inn in this faraway village at the dead end of a mountain road. Plus a young lady with gray eyes set in black lashes and brows —eyes unique in this land of brown eyes. She put the champagne to chill and went back to her task of preparing green beans for dinner.

While the others bathed, I took a vesper walk. The village was only a handful of houses. Perhaps a mile beyond them, on a point of land above the narrowing valley, stood the simple whitewashed church. Evening mists were beginning to blur the outlines of surrounding heights, and a healing silence lay over everything.

Then, floating distinctly across the canyon, came the voices of two human beings. I looked and saw two stooped old people standing in a field, two small dark smudges in the fading pasture. They must have been at least half a mile from me, but, thanks to some happy acoustical accident, their voices were as clear as though they were talking at my elbow. That this distant dialogue was in Basque, of which I could understand not a single word, only enhanced the magic moment.

Our dinner of *piperades* ("tomato omelettes") and *loukinkas* ("little garlic sausages"), chicken, and green salad was washed down with ice-cold champagne and punctuated by toasts to American Independence Day. Our comments on the United States 188 years after—what significance could they have had for the young lady with the gray eyes?

For communion and confirmation Sunday at Ste-Engrâce, people came in from the hills, converging on the tiny white church: old women wearing black scarves and young ones wearing lace mantillas; men dressed in once-a-month suits, white shirts, and black ties, and a few wearing berets.

I'd left Jim and Eve asleep to come up to mass. If ever I had felt out of place it was now. Everyone knew everyone else. Most hadn't seen each other since the last communion a month before. The men stood about on the road, smoking and no doubt discussing shearing, milking, and the price of cheese. The women gathered in the churchyard, gossiping and leaning rather casually, I thought, on the gravestones, and—a few of them—arranging flowers they'd brought for some grave. Near the entrance to the church, an excited class of girls in confirmation white chattered and giggled.

Here was I, in Iowa slacks and shirt and beach-style hat, carrying a camera, knowing not a word of Basque, and feeling like the ghost at the banquet.

Luckily, I spotted the old woman from whom, the previous afternoon, we'd bought the warm pop. Hastening to her side, I greeted her like a former classmate and manufactured conversation with her till the verger pulled the bellrope for all to go in. Taking me under her wing, she ushered me into the church, dipped her fingers in the holy water and crossed herself, then gestured somewhat questioningly to me to do the same. We took our seats on two of the low chairs that doubled as prayer stools.

Young men filed into the gallery at the back. Boys were ranged on benches along one side, the old men on benches that stood on risers under the gallery.

The choice locations, front and center, were for women and girls on their rush-seated chairs. Not that they stayed put! No sooner had my old lady deposited herself than she got up and carried her chair over to where a friend sat. Others moved their chairs about to join friends or to find spots more to their liking. At last, when all were settled, the service began, in Basque. A while later I slipped out.

About Ste-Engrâce Jim had but a single fault to find: the door-knob had come off in his hand, leaving him trapped in his room until I returned from mass and set him free. A trifle.

The young lady did not even bat a gray eye when we offered her a travelers check, telling her it was worth so-and-so many francs. In this sheep country, travelers checks were as unknown as moon rocks, but she took our word. This had happened to us before. The Basques might enjoy the game of smuggling, but in the workaday world they were honest and assumed that others were.

Early the next morning, back at Tardets, having been awakened by a flock of goats bleating under the window, I went to the post office, armed with the family passport, to claim our letters.

"Mais non, Madame," said the postmistress as though she were at least the Prefect of Paris. "Il faut que votre mari vienne aussi." I explained that if my husband hadn't wanted me to get his mail, he wouldn't have given me the passport. It was my authorization.

I was wasting my time and grammar so I gave up. A French postal clerk behind his *guichet* seems to feel the equal of St. Peter.

After a final balcony breakfast, we all assaulted the post office. She handed Jim the letters which turned out to be for me after all.

"Ah, je m'excuse," she apologized. She had thought "Mrs." stood for Monsieur.

Often, as we snacked on bread and cheese and pop in some cool cafe, we'd have for company at a nearby table, workmen of some sort, eating their noon dinner of several courses. A big loaf, round or long, of golden crusted French bread usually came first to the bare wooden table, with the unlabeled, corked-but-not-sealed bottle of *vin ordinaire*. Before the soup arrived, out would come the pocket-knives, each man cutting off a piece of bread to suit his appetite.

It was at Montory, just before we left Soule, the last Basque department, that we saw a bronzed and sweaty laborer cut the sign of the cross into the loaf before cutting a slice from it.

Though demarcations are vague, by the end of the day we knew we were in Béarn. Our Basque walk was over. The balance sheet was mixed.

Pelota games we'd seen (though we had yet to see our best one). *Cuisine eskuarienne* we'd tasted. The Basque language we'd heard. Basque courtesy, Basque cider, Basque mass we'd experienced. A Basque *juerga* we'd witnessed. Basque flutes and drums we'd heard. Basque espadrilles and a Basque beret we'd acquired. Basque cattle flies we'd been bitten by.

But we hadn't seen the *zamalzain*, that dance around and over the wine glass. A *pastorale* we'd seen only in a photograph. We hadn't heard the Basque cry, the *irrintzina*, echoing from mountain to mountain. We'd seen no evidence of the alleged Basque belief in witches, nor any roof tile removed to let the soul of a deceased person ascend to heaven. Nor had we bought a *bota*.

"Didn't really want one anyway," Jim decided. "I can just imagine how wine would taste with all that goat hair inside there." That awful goat hair taste, we later learned, was the reason why real wine skin users never actually swallow the wine but instead squirt it into the back of the throat and let it trickle down by gravity, by-passing the taste buds.

All in all, our two weeks in the Basque country left us feeling not wholly strangers to these proud and unique people whose very blood differs from that of other people. At the same time, it left us pleasantly tantalized, yearning to be returning.

RACE PROBLEM

THE beret was still on nearly every male head in Béarn. But within a few days, gone were the whitewashed houses and cheery tile roofs, gone the tidiness. The Béarnais village was the gray of stone, the gray of slate, the brown of manure. Peeks through arched stable doors revealed dark humid stalls, and often, at the back, stairs leading to the human habitation above. Instead of the communal *fronton* for pelota there was the village street for children and their hoops.

The Basques, we decided, had no monopoly on courtesy. It was in Béarn that, when we thanked someone for favors rendered, we first heard the charming reply "C'est normal." To be gracious was normal.

As we worked eastward, the range was getting higher. No Basque trout had been better than the trout of Béarn taken from torrents plunging down Pyrenean mountainsides.

Hundreds of miles of walking seemed to have made us connoisseurs of soup. "Chabrot bien fait supprime un écu de la poche du médecin" is a favorite Béarnais saying ("A well-made *chabrot* is better than a gold piece to the doctor's pocket"). No Basque soup surpassed the Béarnais *chabrot*.

It's more than just a soup. First you rub the bottom of the pot with garlic, then make a soup of vegetables and herbs, in which you cook a good portion of *confit* ("meat or poultry preserved in its own grease"). Cook "until the ladle can stand by itself in the pot," then serve the whole thing over a slice of bread. When everything's consumed except a bit of broth at the bottom of the soup plate, pour in a glass of red wine and drink the mixture out of the plate. Voilà le chabrot!

A pharmacist had told us to expect lots of greasy food in Béarn. Graisse jusqu'au coude ("grease elbow deep"). We didn't see that it was greasier than, for example, the *confit de canard,* back at Col d'Osquich.

It took us two good *cols* to get over into the valley of the Aspe. There at a fork in the road, hot and tired, we paused to talk with a hydroelectrical engineer. He explained that the torrents coming down from near the frontier were exploited several times in their descent. Counting down from the summit, this plant at Asasp was the fourth of five on the River Aspe.

The tremendous hydroelectric resources of the Aspe notwithstanding, we were in the land of the dim bulb. The hotel where we set down for the night at Lurbe was like most Pyrenean hotels: two forty-watt bulbs for one big room. Or sometimes it was one live seventy-five-watt bulb and one dead one. (Evidently they trusted you wouldn't have the gumption to ask for a replacement.)

Madame showed us a room containing twin beds and a crib. After some lame jokes about who was to sleep in the crib, we waited for her to show us a second room. She had reserved this double for Jim and me and for Eve a single room in the village.

"I'll take the room in the village," Jim offered gallantly.

"Why shouldn't I take it?" said Eve. "It's for me."

"It's a pig in a poke anyway," Jim decided. "Let's just make do, the three of us, here."

Our hostess, when we told her our decision, gave a Gallic shrug that said, "What can you expect from Americans crazy enough to go on foot?"

So, with recollections of another night eight years before in Gournay, Eve and I prepared once more to disprove that preposterous law that says two bodies cannot occupy the same space at the same time.

The Tour de France was the topic of conversation in a farmhouse where we stopped the next day for a midmorning break. The woman served us our pop and brought out plates and knives when she saw we had not only bread and cheese but peaches. She then went ahead with serving *déjeuner* to her husband, his field helper, and herself.

The cyclists, the man told us, would be going past that afternoon on the big highway not far away. If we could get to Arudy and cross the River Ossau to the highway by four o'clock, he was certain we could see them ride by. With high hopes we packed up our knapsacks and started on.

Not only had we for years seen newsreels of the Tour de France, but Jim and I felt we were part of the worldwide bicycle brotherhood. The year after we were married—long before the current bike craze in the United States—we'd made a seventy-one-hundred-mile tandem bicycle trip from Pacific to Atlantic and back to the Pacific. A purely fun trip, it had nevertheless set a couple of records in 1938: the longest tandem trip ever made in America and the longest mixed-couple tandem trip ever made anywhere. So although these cyclists were professionals, or perhaps because they were, we wanted (Jim especially) to lay eyes on them in the flesh.

While people rushed past us in cars, on *motos,* and on bicycles, all hurrying to see the race, we plodded patiently on.

The woods were cool but the climb was steady, the kilometers many, and the wild blackberries irresistible. From Arudy we could see crowds lining the highway nearly a mile away across the river. A news helicopter hovered overhead. It was already after four. Clearly, we couldn't walk over there in time to see the cyclists pass.

"Let's taxi over and then come back here to pick up our trail," proposed Jim. "That won't spoil our record any more than taking the funicular up La Rhune and back spoiled it."

There existed but one taxi in Arudy, and it was *occupé*. Defeated, we sat down at a sidewalk table and ordered some ice cream. We could even hear the crowd cheering now.

"If you women hadn't insisted on that last berry stop," he grumbled, "we might have gotten the taxi. We might be over there by now."

"Here," I said on a sudden inspiration. "Look through this." I handed him my camera, with telephoto lens in place. He admitted he saw a cyclist ride past.

"It was partly my fault about the berries," Eve apologized. "Here, take my fronton." (Our name for the cookie that was almost always stuck perpendicularly, like the wall of a pelota court, into the ice cream.) In the face of such sacrifice, Jim's love gauge swung far to the positive, and all was well.

But the end of an Army-Navy game could hardly have turned loose on the surrounding countryside a wilder traffic melee than eventuated now that the race had passed. Tired, short-tempered people in cars and on motorcyles tried to extricate themselves and get where they were going. Tired, short-tempered children wearing paper hats that said "Orangina" had to be silenced, dragged across streets, spanked. Tired, short-tempered gendarmes tried to untangle the snarl.

Jostled, honked at, and given dirty looks, we felt almost as though we had really been to the Tour de France.

Even more "been to it" were the Belgian family we got acquainted with that evening. They'd had no intention of spending the night there at Izeste. Not being French, they hadn't even been thinking of the race. But because of the crowds, the police had required them to stop there!

A good thing we had wanted to sleep at Izeste. For had any French gendarme tried to push us around like that, our American concept of personal freedom might have given us an intimate glimpse of a Béarnais jail.

PRIME CLIMB

A NEARLY abandoned road up the valley of the Ossau gave us tranquility, distant views of the valley with its farms marked off by stone walls and near views of Béarnais village life.

In Béon, women were washing at the communal washing place. A girl, riding past on her bicycle, reached back to break off a mouthful of bread from the loaf strapped to the luggage carrier. A cat reigned in solitary somnolence in a hall where on Saturday nights there used to be dances to accordion music.

It was cold and damp, and someone suggested a soup stop at Aste.

We'd thought every good Pyrenean housewife always had *potage* on the back of the stove, but Aste had no soup ready. Madame more than made up for her souplessness by showing us Béarnais flutes and *tambourins*. Like the Basque flutes, these Béarnais flutes had three holes and were end blown. One of the *tambourins* dated from the sixteenth century and the other was a modern copy of it: a long wooden box with six heavy gut strings. The flutes and the replica *tambourin* were going to be used the coming weekend at Laruns.

Passing under the hamlet of Ans that hung on a crag like an eagle's nest, we were suddenly in Eaux-Bonnes. Here, at our first Pyrenean spa, at this small town crowded on a steep wall of the Valentin gorge, we took our second layover.

Being healthy, we'd always shied away from spas. The idea of a community whose economy is geared to ailments of the liver, stomach, kidneys, skin, and/or intestines did not appeal to us. In a hotel full of sick people, whatever table conversation we could overhear would probably be a lively discussion of whether a certain dish was *bon pour* or *pas bon pour* the stomach. With our walking trip appetites, we preferred to enjoy our meals without thought of physiology.

But we needed a cleanup, and you can count on a spa for rooms with private baths and ample space to hang a good batch of wash.

Dinner the night of our arrival dispelled all fears. If these people tucking away three-thousand-calorie dinners in utter, serious silence were sick, I'd hate to have to provision the well. Mostly families, three and even four generations of hearty, energetic bourgeois, they far outdid even the Youngs, who'd walked seventeen kilometers uphill. Soup, paté, roast, vegetables, potatoes, salad, cheese, fruit, pastry—all accompanied by a quantity of French bread and washed down with red wine. (The children, we were glad to note, drank milk, or water with a bit of wine added.)

No, these people were just vacationers. Eaux-Bonnes still had its thermal establishment where people could take baths in the good waters *(eaux bonnes)*. But it was now primarily a resort town. The more vigorous guests could play tennis and take real walks. For the less robust, there was a *promenade horizontale* ("flat walk"). And there was the casino and there were countless sidewalk cafes at which to take on another few calories between meals in the form of drinks, pastry, ice cream, or hot chocolate. We had the sense that Eaux-Bonnes was past its prime.

Recklessness, born of the knowledge we'd walked 183 miles in fifteen days, overcame us.

and a picnic or a meal at the restaurant if there is one, is a favorite outing. That is, for those who live and work in town. Many farmers spend their Sundays in cafes, drinking and playing cards.

As we started down we met amateur cyclists cheerfully laboring up the *col* where the professionals had passed in the race earlier.

In the Cirque du Litor beside a spring, a shepherd, an old redhead, had just finished doing his laundry in the ice-cold spring water and was filling a big milk can to carry to his hut some distance away. Tall, thin, and bright eyed, he had about a five-tooth smile.

"Est-ce que l'eau est bonne?" was our rather silly opener. Of course the water was good!

"C'est l'eau de ciel," was his reply. ("It's the water of heaven.") There were two hundred sheep in his flock, he said, and he made half a ton of cheese every year.

After we left him we began to wonder. "Eau de ciel" was a more poetic expression than we'd have expected from a simple shepherd—the water of heaven, heavenly water! "Could it mean 'rainwater'?" Eve asked. "That would be water from heaven." It could, we decided, and yet we'd seen the water trickling into a concrete trough from a pipe that came out of the mountain—our conception of a spring. It was all very confusing, and when we were finally able to confirm that Eve's guess was right, that it did mean rainwater, we were still unconvinced about that trough and that pipe.

On the Col de Soulor more French families were enjoying themselves. The descent from there, our guidebook told us, was an ideal section for "amateur picnickers."

"What do you have to do," Eve wondered, "to become a professional picnicker?"

Another shepherd was putting away his big shears. He'd just done some shearing, had put the fleece into a bag and tied it up. Two two-day-old lambs were in his flock, a white and a black.

Near Arrens, burros were at work in the hayfields, and roadside stands advertised cheese and honey, both "of the country." Like good amateur picnickers, we bought cheese for our next day's walk, hoping it had been made by our redheaded friend.

From the Crêtes Blanches we'd descended more than twenty-seven hundred feet. That we were making headway west to east was attested by a towel at the Arrens hotel. It was plainly marked with the name of an Andorra hotel.

A DANGEROUS BULL

"GETTING time for a snack, isn't it?" Jim suggested toward mid-morning. "What's the next village on your map, Binkie?"

I considered. "Aucun."

"You mean there's no village before the end of the day?"

"No, I mean the next village is Aucun."

"A village called 'none'? We can't expect much from that."

Aucun had a cafe, and the cafe had a millstone table on a terrace beside an irrigation canal.

Rare indeed is the French village without its cafe. Each is different, yet the common denominators are so common that in any cafe we always felt at home at once and near to the village pulse.

Whether it's simply a bare, dark room in the *cafetier*'s residence, or a more sophisticated establishment with terrace, umbrella tables, and perhaps a flower box or two, the cafe plays a prime role in village life.

Here the farmer or worker stops in at day's end for a glass of red wine and a bit of talk with friends. Here the child is sent, carrying an empty bottle to be filled with wine for the noon meal. Here old men while away a Sunday, playing cards or reading, gratis, the provincial newspaper—over very little in the way of drinks. Here the smoker may buy tobacco, matches, a lighter; the schoolteacher may buy postage stamps; the optimist, lottery tickets.

The cafe may possess the only telephone in the village. Seldom is anyone better informed than the owner. He or his wife will relate to any who inquire how so-and-so's sick mother is doing, what the latest rumor is about the sale of such-and-such land, and who made the week's best score at *pétanque* (the French version, with balls, of horseshoes).

Though some idle men (mostly middle-aged or old ones) may spend the better part of every day at the cafe, they're masters of the art of attenuated drinking. Almost never did we see drunkenness in a French cafe.

Depending on the hour—and we stopped in at all hours—the cafe might be crowded or deserted. When there was a crowd, we delighted in watching and eavesdropping while we ate and drank. When we were alone with the proprietor, he or she would usually pump us, in order to regale the habitués with details about us later on.

Mademoiselle, the barmaid of Aucun, when she learned we were Americans, wondered if we knew her uncle in Oceanview, California. It was hard for her to realize that California alone is three-fourths the size of the whole of France.

Market day, and that day the day before Bastille Day. Argelès was teeming. It's a two-part town. On the upper level stands the original town with its accretions of centuries. At one side there's a steep dropoff, over which, one fine day long ago, some irate Argelésiens threw the tax collector. Down there now is the thermal establishment —park, baths, spring house, cafe, casino, and cinema.

Not only a market town, Argelès is a crossroads for two of the most visited spots in the Pyrenees. To the north, only thirteen kilometers away, is Lourdes, where every year nearly two million visitors and pilgrims go. More than to Rome, Jerusalem, or Mecca! To the southeast, some thirty-eight kilometers, is the Cirque de Gavarnie, acknowledged the most dramatic scenic feature of the French Pyrenees. Gavarnie we'd have loved, without its thousands of visitors.

Busload after charter busload bound for Lourdes and bound for Gavarnie told us we'd been right to omit those places from our plans. Either of those spots on or around July 14 would have been impossible.

It was a hot, hot, hot Bastille Day. Even on our back road traffic was heavy. Picnickers were everywhere, complete with their tables, chairs, dinnerware, linen. (Perhaps the full regalia made them professionals?) As for us, we snacked here on a shady wall, there in a cool tunnel.

Walking ahead of us as we approached Luz in the late afternoon sunshine was a family of five, three full-size rakes and two small rakes over five shoulders. When there's hay to be turned, the Pyrenean farmer will take his family into the field and, ordinarily, work there until near dark, the children with their pint-size rakes working alongside their parents, and all stopping briefly for supper in the field. But this family had knocked off two or three hours early. It was Bastille Day, and they couldn't resist the fireworks which they knew would be part of the celebration.

By seven-thirty the streets of Luz were swarming with the holiday crowd. On the square, just across the bridge from where we were dining, a six-piece band from Spain was tuning up, and people were gathering to listen. We followed the crowd and found good standing room in front of a low parking barrier. While daylight faded and night came on, Roger Garcia's combo played some jazz *à l'espagnol.*

P—ssh—bang! Rockets went off over the bandstand. The music stopped and the fireworks got started in earnest.

From somewhere there appeared a life-size bull made of plywood. I recalled having seen it pass us that afternoon, atop someone's car.

One man was inside, prancing *el toro* around the square, while another more or less led him to avert disaster. For this was *el toro de fuego,* the Spanish fire-bull, and he was covered with fireworks that sputtered, changed color, fizzed, sparkled, and exploded as he cavorted.

Whenever he approached the crowd, there were delighted screams as people backed away. He came toward us, and with one accord the three of us backed away, all falling down. We'd forgotten the six-inch-high parking barrier at our heels.

Next, what appeared to be mere street decorations just above our heads—bunting, pennants, and the like—began to go off. It all wound up with street dancing, during which long snakes of youngsters kept running pell-mell through the crowd.

Why no one was blinded, burned, or even (except us) bruised, must have been due to some conscientious guardian angel charged with looking after people menaced by bulls, fireworks, and heedless children.

BÉARN BEHIND, BIGORRE BEFORE

THE reputation of Col du Tourmalet, highest *col* in the French Pyrenees, had inspired in us some apprehension, so to get a good look at it we rode the cable railway from Barèges up the flank of Pic d'Ayré. The *col* rose even higher than the upper end of the funicular, and we could see it fairly sizzling in the July sun.

We took a big breath, took some pictures, took the funicular back down. Once more safe in Barèges, Jim confided he'd noticed one of the cables was badly worn. "It was frayed, and I was 'fraid too."

Hardly a tree graced the four-hours-plus climb up Tourmalet. But the road was cut right into the mountainside, and now and then when the switchback switched the right way we found ourselves in the blessed shadow of the mountain itself. At one such spot a cool draft issued from a crack in the rock, and it was hard to tear ourselves away.

True to form, French families were disporting themselves on the *col*, picking flowers, taking each other's pictures, and—naturally—lifting fork and glass to lips.

We were at ninety-three hundred feet above sea level. Off to the north a few short miles towered the Pic du Midi de Bigorre, but we felt we'd climbed enough for one day. Besides, we could see forever from where we already were—back into the Béarn we were leaving and on into the Bigorre ahead.

Like the Basques and the Béarnais, the Bigourdans were renowned for driving a hard political bargain. They agreed to let the seigneur rule them only if he'd guarantee their rights and privileges. "Sinon, non" ("if not, no")! They fought the English in the fifteenth century and greedy Finance Minister Colbert and his salt tax in the seventeenth. Bigorre had had a number of female rulers—doughty women, some of them.

On the other side of Tourmalet was an amazing establishment, an Albigensian center. The Albigensians (in a sense precursors of the Reformation, for they objected to the clergy's vices) followed a belief of Oriental origin. In the Middle Ages they had become so strong in southern France that finally Pope Innocent in the thirteenth century instituted what amounted to a crusade against them. Persecution lasted on and off for decades, down to 1244, when, it was believed, the last Albigensians were wiped out.

Yet here they were, alive and well, and living in a refuge on the slopes of Tourmalet!

Not far from their refuge, in the shadow of a ski lift at La Mongie, we found a ski lodge open. Small, simple, and simply heaven to three tired Americans.

Tramp, tramp, tramp! We started down the valley of the Gripp, a small stream that was visible twisting far ahead as it glanced in the morning sun. An invisible band was playing in our heads saying: *You've come over the highest pass in the French Pyrenees. From here on it's got to be all downhill.* Irrational but pleasant.

At the first village downmountain, in a modest family hotel, *pensionnaires* were starting off their noon meal with some of the most gorgeous hors d'oeuvres it had ever been our misfortune to see. But every hard-cooked egg, every tomato slice, every anchovy, every radish, every olive, and every pickle had been counted and computed. There were exactly enough for the *pensionnaires*, but not a morsel more. We would have to wait for replenishments.

Drooling while waiting, we examined the stuffed head of an isard, the Pyrenean chamois, and some old fox traps in a closet. They no longer trapped foxes around here, but hunters did occasionally bring back an isard. How anyone could shoot such a mild-eyed little creature was beyond us.

There were more sabots than espadrilles now; and thatched roofs, which had first appeared as we came down off Tourmalet, continued as we struck up the valley of the Adour. Enclosed courtyards and recessed porches, too, told us we were in the heart of Bigorre. Beyond Payolle, we rested under a beech tree near a marble quarry at whose entrance were ten samples of local marble of ten distinct colors.

It was another hot *col* climb, and, just over the top, a cafe advertised crêpes. Being only human, we ordered crêpes.

We waited. . . . *There are customers indoors too. Maybe they ordered first. . . . She probably has a griddle only just so big. . . .*

They've gone to town for butter. . . . They're looking up the recipe.
. . . The guy who makes them is having a drink. . . . Finally they
came: three diminutive crêpes that any one of us could have consumed in ten seconds, blindfolded and with hands tied behind the
back.

Next time we'd wire ahead, for crêpes *pour douze personnes.*

(The magic word "crêpes" beguiled us a day or so later, but,
we were twenty-five minutes early. They did not make crêpes before
twelve o'clock. Battles have been lost, have they not, because of such
punctilio?)

"Hope you have an easy day for us tomorrow, Binkie," Jim said
as we settled down for the night at Arreau.

I hemmed and hawed a bit.

"Eve," he said, "you were looking at the map. What kind of
day do we have?"

She looked questioningly at me.

"You guessed it, Jim," I said. "Another *col.*" We'd climbed
three major *cols* in the eight days since our last layover. "But Peyrasourde is only 1,536 meters above sea level."

"You're quoting it in meters so it'll sound lower, eh?"

"Not at all. It's just a shade over five thousand feet. For people
who've been over Tourmalet—"

"And Aubisque," added Eve.

"And umpteen others," I continued. "For people like us, it'll
be a snap."

There was a troubled quality about his snoring that night, but
we rose, all three in good spirits, and, while church bells rang, filed
out of Arreau.

The sun was getting high when, somewhere off in a field, a
farmer spied us and sang out with French accent the opening phrase
of doubtless the only English song he knew. "It's a long way to
Tipperary . . ."

"It's a long way to go," Jim sang back to him. And I knew that,
after all, I was not really in bad.

On Col de Peyrasourde, people were scrambling around the
rocky meadows gathering what looked like giant dandelions. We'd
seen these ugly things before on *cols,* and seen them, dried, as wall
decorations.

A grizzled shepherd on the *col* carried a sack made of fleece slung
from his shoulder, and a few minutes' conversation made it clear
that the sack contained liquid refreshment. Had it not been for his
bright and capering dog, a teetotaler, this man's flock would have

gotten widely separated, drowned, fallen over cliffs, been eaten by wolves.

Once more the *col* was a kind of milestone. Behind lay Bigorre; ahead lay Comminges, and in Comminges was the watershed between Atlantic and Mediterranean. We'd walked more than 270 miles from St-Jean-de-Luz. To the north a sun-burnished peak floated like an island in a sea of fog. Below us a row of trees began to emerge from the creamy mist. Somewhere sheep bleated.

We were nearing still another historic route over the mountains to Santiago de Compostela, this one over the Port de Vénasque—a more difficult route by far than Roncevaux. If we did nothing else in the Pyrenees, had been our resolve before leaving home, we would get to Hospice de France, the tiny inn in the mountains, at the foot of Vénasque. In the eleventh century it had been a stopping place for pilgrims bound for Santiago. Because the inn could accommodate only five persons, we'd made reservations a month earlier from St-Jean-de-Luz.

As a foretaste of the hospice—now a favorite center for mountain climbers—we made the acquaintance, a few kilometers before Luchon, of an aged former mountain guide. A tight beret topped his white hair, and a red sash was wound round his waist. He wore black rope-soled shoes. His face was bronzed and deeply lined, and his leathery hands were twisted and knobby.

Our undertaking won his approval and loosened his tongue. After a lengthy dissertation on the health benefits of walking and climbing, he modestly admitted that because he'd spent all his eighty-some years in the mountains, he possessed *un moral parfait* ("perfect mental powers").

He must have been a cousin of the hunter whose trophies we ran into a few days later. Posted beneath the head and one foot of an isard, the head and several feet of a wild boar, and the horn of a mountain sheep, was a card, in French, stating bashfully: Shot By You Know Whom.

Liberté, égalité, fraternité, yes. *Humilité?* No.

BOWL AND PITCHER PARADISE

IT was ten days now since we'd had a full day's layover. We were entitled to be lazy at Luchon before the climb to Hospice de France.

Though Luchon's waters are said to be great for tired vocal cords, we saw not a single singer, preacher, professor, orator, entertainer, lawyer, politician, nor any other customer enter or leave the thermal establishment or *vaporarium*.

Luchon, like Eaux-Bonnes, had only well guests in evidence. They strolled the gravel walks of formal parks, strolled colonnades where it was "absolutely forbidden" to play ball, strolled avenues where expensive *salons de thé* glittered with crystal and mirrors. They played tennis, golf, miniature golf, *pétanque*. They flew model airplanes, sat knitting and gossiping on park benches, swam in the *piscine*. Children played ball, rolled hoops, took donkey rides.

Biggest treat for us was a fast game between professional pelota teams of Luchon and nearby Bagnères de Bigorre. The six men moved about the large court so swiftly that, but for their sashes of red and of black, it would have been impossible to follow the game.

The small ball, with rubber center, a layer of wool, and a tight cover of dogskin, sometimes travels more than 150 miles per hour. No wonder the front wall has to be built of granite instead of concrete! All in one motion, the player scoops it out of the air with his *chistera,* lets it roll down toward his hand, then returns it to the wall with terrific force. Several times, when no one got the ball as it came from the front wall, it traveled clear to the back wall and bounced off it. Then one of the players who'd missed it would catch it and return it to the front wall. To give it the necessary "oomph" on this play, he'd often throw himself to the concrete floor.

This was handball to the "*n*th" power. These professionals far surpassed in grace, agility, and endurance the remarkable displays we'd seen among youngsters and amateurs along our way in the Basque country.

Through it all, the *chacharia,* or scorekeeper, called out the points, sometimes getting a good laugh from the spectators by inserting humorous impromptu couplets about the players. If only we'd been enough in the know to laugh with them!

The profile map said the climb to Hospice de France would attain an 18 percent grade. As far as we knew, that would be the steepest we'd climbed on any route intended for car travel. But what might daunt drivers certainly didn't daunt us.

At first a fair road and then a narrow rutty track carried us up through beautiful beech and pine forests. Steeper and steeper it got.

There came an irregular crashing and thudding, and a huge boulder that would have demolished a car thundered down the steep hillside, missed us by perhaps twenty feet, and catapulted on down the bank.

By midafternoon we stood in probably the most enchanting spot of our experience: a meadow watered by melting glaciers and surrounded by ridges and peaks, some forested, some bare and jag-toothed. Before us, the hospice: of stone, nestling small and snug, with a barn at one side.

Madame Renée Haurillon, red haired, handsome, and friendly, greeted us by name. She and her husband were expecting us.

The stairs and floors were worn deep and silken smooth. Our two connecting rooms on the second floor looked out on the forbidding mountains that guarded the Spanish frontier. Furnishings were clean, in good repair, very simple. Far from our first, or last, bowl and pitcher place, it then and there won our deepest affection.

In a sunroom, beside a stuffed bear, we chatted before dinner with Monsieur Haurillon's father.

He'd lived up there since childhood, had until recent years taken parties of alpinists on hazardous ascents and cross-country expeditions. He'd hunted the isard, the fox, and the eagle. The bear we were looking at he'd captured when it was a month-old cub, and had kept it at the hospice until, when it was eighteen months old, a jealous competitor poisoned it. Heartbroken, he'd had it stuffed, to keep it always near him.

The stuffed bear, the old man, and his story of the cub all seemed pretty real and immediate to us. Little did we guess how much more real and immediate a certain bear was going to seem to us within a week.

Though part of the *hostellerie,* including our rooms, was more recent, the dining room was essentially as it had been in the eleventh century when pilgrims stopped here for food and warmth and shelter. The woodwork was dark, the floor stone. Two cosy seats flanked the fireplace where a fire crackled. Its glow was reflected by brass and copper kettles and utensils along the walls where also hung isard heads and autographed pictures of celebrities.

Madame Haurillon had prepared for us a typical Pyrenean *garbure,* a soup of vegetables, chicken, and sego. One of the secrets of a good *garbure* being the *mijotage,* the long slow cooking, she must have started it while we were still in Luchon.

"If we were smart," said I, "we'd vow never again to eat soup of any kind, because nothing will ever come up to this."

Then came a tripe stew, of lamb tripe with potatoes, curry, bay leaves, and stock. It, too, had been simmered a long time. Good red wine accompanied both it and the lamb chops which Monsieur grilled at the fireplace. Green salad. And crêpes. Delicious crêpes. Enough of them. And no waiting for them.

Night was falling, and we joined Monsieur outside to watch the mist envelop the mountains and hide the early stars. He and his father, he told us, used to make cross-country trips on skis, sometimes being away several days.

"How old is your father?"

"He's the oldest living mountain guide in France—eighty-four."

"I'm sure he has always lived a very healthy life."

"In summer, you could track where he had gone, anywhere in the mountains, just by looking for his cigarette stubs."

"If the Marquis de Rozel could get artillery pieces up there in 1711," Jim declared, looking up toward Vénasque the next morning, "we-uns ought to be able to get ourselves up there today."

Wildflowers galore, including miniature annunciation lilies, brightened the now-and-then muletrack. Smaller and smaller looked the hospice below. More and more we felt like goats as we scrambled up rocks, balanced and clambered, vaulted, and once or twice slid.

Finally, about noon, we reached snow level; in a spot the sun seldom got to, there was a patch of *névé,* old granulated snow. Far above us, a ribbon of water dropped over the lip of a cliff—the head-waters of the Pique.

But to get to the top was out of the question. Jim had missed his Tour de France. Eve still didn't have her Spanish shawl, and I must now forgo a much desired sight of the Maladeta Range of Spain. So near and yet so far!

With a last wistful glance up, we started back, for the Haurillons were expecting us for lunch. What was more, we'd promised Luchon television people they could interview and photograph us, and they were sending a truck to meet us. A promise was a promise.

Monsieur had prepared a delicious *gigot à la ficelle,* a leg of mutton which hung from the chimney, twisting and untwisting over the coals.

Nervous because we thought we were going to have to talk on television, we ate hurriedly, paid up, and made our adieus to the three Haurillons. In only about twenty-four hours, this place and these people had struck a chord of utter harmony in our hearts.

GAIN A SHAWL, LOSE A NAPKIN

AS soon as we saw that the young man from the television station wasn't taping, but simply taking notes, the interview went well. The rest was simple: just letting the photographer shoot us as we walked trails, crossed a footbridge. As we started down that 18 percent grade, they preceded us in low gear, filming from the tailgate.

Off they went then, to cover a judo match, and once more the beech forest was ours: silent but for the sound of birds, of a distant axe, and our footsteps.

The rose in the hair—the fringed shawl—the man beneath the balcony, strumming his guitar—Eve was enchanted by the lure of nearby Spain. Burguete had been a mere teaser. La Rhune was so brief it didn't count at all. Even I, who had been in Spain years before, wanted more.

"I wouldn't have any objection to Spain," Jim had said, "if it were a French-speaking country. But we'll go if only to get that Spanish shawl," he promised.

Adelante! On our way! It would be another long hot climb, from Luchon again but up a different pass. Once over the Col du Portillon, we'd be in Spain.

Past a fish hatchery and past two sets of French border guards. Past a big lumber depot and into a beech forest where toyon and holly abounded. Canteen refills at springs that came out of rocks and at *eau potable* pipes. . . .

Early afternoon found us at the Spanish frontier station atop the *col*, better than forty-five hundred feet elevation. Beyond, as the view opened, were massive, forbidding, barren mountains—Spain. The unsatisfied ache I'd felt at Vénasque was gone, or nearly gone. For although I'd had my heart set on the harder route, it was no small thing to have gotten here all by ourselves on our own six feet.

A few kilometers down from the summit, two soldiers in green uniforms, with guns, were crouched in the brush near the road.

I raised my camera. "Con su permiso?"

"No."

What or whom were they waiting for?

"You wanted to come to Spain," Jim exulted. "That's your Franco Spain for you!" The faint anxiety in my heart was quickly overshadowed by a strong sense of the romantic fitness of those mysterious *guardias* in this semiarid, semisavage spot.

By contrast, hundreds of feet below us, the Val d'Aran lay flat and verdant, with neatly tended farms climbing the lower slopes. Switchback after switchback took us down the mountainside. Any additional soldiers in ambush were better hidden than the first two. We saw no more.

At a second frontier station on the outskirts of Bosost, a type right out of the movies sat in an elegantly carved armchair on a colonnade, ready to stamp our passport. Nearby, a group of road-workers were doing something vague to the street, and when they saw my camera they hastened to strike a pose. It was almost identical with the pose struck by those other roadworkers above Roncevaux: man with raised sledgehammer prepares to slaughter fellow worker. This was Spanish humor again.

There was time, before nine o'clock dinner, for a walk, shop, and snack-aperitif. The walk was through picturesque back alleys and along the great Garonne River, a mighty stream, wide, deep, and strong. Ripley would have liked, perhaps did like and feature in his "Believe It Or Not" series, the Garonne. High up in the mountains above Bosost is a small glacial stream which by all rights should empty into the Spanish river Ebro. The lay of the land places it definitely in the Mediterranean watershed. But French speleologist Norbert Caste-ret suspected otherwise. By adding dye high up there where the small glacial stream disappears into a hole, he proved that it runs about four kilometers underground and issues forth eighteen hundred feet lower, joining the Garonne, which empties into the Atlantic.

The shop—to buy at long last the Spanish shawl, a beauty and perhaps the only Spanish shawl ever carried any distance in a knap-sack.

The snack-aperitif was served by a boy not older than ten.

Posted in one of our rooms was a card in English. "If you have any complaints or suggestions, please write them in the book pro-vided for the purpose." So far, so good. But it was headed "Caution."

As it had taken two French and two Spanish frontier stations to get us into Spain, it now took two more of each, along the Garonne, to get us back into France. The river, mighty at Bosost, shrank to modest proportions thanks to a hydroelectric plant, then roared on at full volume once more. The valley flattened out then narrowed again and the sun beat down like an open blast furnace.

Known long ago as *"la clef de la France"* because it commanded this southern portal, St-Béat is cramped tight as key in keyhole by the walls of the Garonne valley. How tight is shown by flood levels recorded on the main street: in 1897, before hydroelectric days, the river had risen a good six feet above the sidewalk.

On the outskirts of the village of Chaum, five men in their Sun-day best stood in a front yard, playing saxophone, clarinet, accordion, trumpet, and guitar. We waved and went on. To our surprise, they left the yard, walked a few rods, turned in at another yard, and played another few merry measures. Thus, all the way to Chaum they trailed close behind us making music.

When we stopped at the village cafe, they stopped too, for this was what it was all about. They'd been giving a musical come-on for a community celebration. They settled down to playing and the villagers settled down to drinking and listening. As we left the valley of the Sunday musicians, the mountains of Spain brooded at our backs.

By now, *La Dépêche du Midi* had run its illustrated article on our pedestrian exploits. Those who read the more cosmopolitan *Figaro* from Paris had perhaps seen us described in a thirteen-line paragraph as three *fervents* of walking. And finally, airing of the television featurette completed the job. We were semipublic figures, and people waved to us in a friendly spirit.

At Fronsac, shortly before we were to tackle another *col*, a cafe owner who'd read about us invited us to sit at a family table in the side arbor instead of out at a sidewalk table. A former alpinist and mountain guide, he'd served the highest postal route in France. After suffering a double fracture, he'd had to give up his strenuous work. He was well read, especially in Chateaubriand, but he'd apparently skimmed the article about the American family walking coast to coast *en guise de vacances*. For he thought we were English and that we were averaging forty kilometers a day. The truth, to this point, was more like seventeen.

"Forty kilometers was probably a mere stroll to him when he was active," Jim observed wistfully as we went on our way.

It was hot, and the drinks our guide friend had served us were soon forgotten in a new thirst. Partway up Col des Ares we decided that, since we had several kilometers of climbing ahead of us, it would be nice to sit in the shade and cut that luscious-smelling melon I'd bought in St-Béat. As we refreshed ourselves with its sweet juiciness, we could hear talk and laughter coming through the trees from, we supposed, picnickers.

Not five minutes beyond our melon stop, we found ourselves at La Palombière, where we had reservations. Though we'd been told it was at the top of the pass, it was nearly five kilometers short of the summit—to a motorized person, nothing.

It was the midday diners at La Palombière that we'd heard, but they soon departed, and all was quiet for the countdown till dinner time.

Of all the odd bathrooms we've used on walking trips, the one at La Palombière was the most touching. For it doubled as the servant girl's bedroom.

In it was her narrow, downhill bed; in it was a cramped wardrobe containing her few clothes; in it, for some reason, was a ladder; and stuck into the freckled mirror were the pictures she prized of family and friends. In it, one felt very much an intruder.

Dinner was served on the veranda. About the time the sautéed kidneys arrived, I could see menacing clouds over Spain, and by the time we'd finished them, La Palombière was shrouded in darkness. Awnings and sun umbrellas were flapping wildly and vacant chairs were blowing over. The management rushed out to save things.

I took my wineglass and the bread; Eve, her wineglass and the water carafe; Jim, his wineglass and the wine bottle. The remaining things were rescued by Madame and the *jeune fille* who slept in the bathroom, and we all went indoors just as Jim's napkin took wing over the valley of the Garonne.

MAMA'S STOMACH DOES FLIP-FLOPS

IT'S strange how the inflections of one's mother tongue will ring familiarly on the ear long before words are distinguishable. Beyond Col des Ares we were sitting beside the road eating croissants left from our super-plentiful breakfast when two distant male voices broke into our consciousness. We pricked up our ears. It was, it must be English!

Over the summit came two cyclists, Messrs. Carter and Parry of London, England. They were having a "fortnight's holiday" on their Raleigh "wheels." They were our kind. They strongly agreed when Jim said, "If modern life doesn't provide us with hardship, we must seek it." Presently, with a "cheerio," they sped off down the hill, leaving with us an Anglo-Saxon glow.

The storm of the previous night had cleared the air. Ahead of us, as we followed our British cousins down the steep descent, was wooded, green, sixty-two-hundred-foot Pic de Cagire, a mountain sacred to the Romans. Scattered near and far were tile-roofed villages. Their warm color spoke to us of our objective, the Mediterranean.

The Massif d'Arbas is a jumble of calcareous mountains riddled with caves and—witness the odd behavior of the Garonne headwaters—underground rivers. Under the plateau of Juzet, that same speleologist, Norbert Casteret, had discovered in 1931 a series of remarkable caves at different levels. In the forties, a group of Paris spelunkers had found and explored the abyss of Henne-Morte, going down to about 1,450 feet.

We talked of these and other things with a young carpenter-mason at Juzet. This youthful artisan not only introduced himself and his wife to us, but he introduced us to a favorite beverage of the Midi workman: the tango, a beer with grenadine syrup added. If a taste for the tango is a prerequisite, I'm afraid I'll never join the Midi working class.

In the lovely wooded gorge of the Ger, prelude to still another *col*, a plaque above a hole in the cliff spelled out: James Brace, *Spéléologue*. The entrance would have been an impossible squeeze for any of us. It was sobering to imagine how the comrades of this jockey-built English cave enthusiast must have pulled him out feet first, dead or dying. Issuing from the opening were visible, noxious fumes. With one accord we voted to leave speleology to braver souls.

The road, steep and very narrow, was without traffic. Presently, a car containing a middle-aged couple came up from behind and stopped beside us.

"Voulez-vous monter?" the man asked. Would we like to get in?

We were walking for pleasure, we explained, and for the health benefits of it. (Of late we'd been adding the *bénéfices* bit, having noticed that the French could accept that idea more readily than mere pleasure.)

"Alors, donnez-nous vos bagages." We declined to give them our baggage, explaining that this would have been against our principles.

"Mais la route est très dure. Treize pour cent sur trois kilomètres." But the road was very difficult—a 13 percent grade for three kilometers.

We thanked them *quand même*.

All the way up, we kept expecting them to pass us but they never did. Evidently they'd somehow managed to turn around and had gone back down. They'd driven up for no other reason than to offer us a ride!

Was it the couple from Henne-Morte? On the outskirts of that village we'd noticed such a charming house with a table under such a beautiful flowering vine that, though we saw no sign or license, we thought it might be a cafe. Of a woman at the window we asked "Est-ce que c'est ici un café?"

"Non," but would we like to come in and cool off?

Having put her on the spot that way, we couldn't accept.

Could it be, now, that she and her husband had driven after us purposely to give us a lift up the *col*?

Or were they a couple who'd seen us on television and had bet on whether or not we'd accept a ride? An enigma for the ages.

A place called Chez Martin, supposed to be on Col du Portet d'Aspet, had accepted our reservations by phone. All we saw, through the deluge that was drenching us as we surmounted the pass, was a small building labeled Chalet des Pyrénées. But the luck of the Youngs held. Chalet des Pyrénées and Chez Martin were one and the same. This was it and they expected us.

Madame Martin led us up a spiral staircase so narrow that our knapsacks scraped. On the second floor she showed us three tiny rooms, each with bowl, pitcher, and slop bucket. That was the entire upstairs of the Chalet des Pyrénées, but it was enough for us.

Downstairs in the dining room, the chalet could have accommodated perhaps twenty. The walls were decorated with the now familiar "dried dandelions" and with pictures and autographs of speleologists.

Reward for our 13 percent climb was a *cassoulet* of white beans and sausage, cooked in earthenware in the fireplace. Said Madame: "Il faut absolument sept fois briser et mélanger à la masse la peau qui se forme au-dessus." That was the key to this arcanum of gourmet cooking. It was nice to know, but if anyone thought I was going to mess around breaking a skin seven times, they had another think coming.

Only in the tiny hall at the head of the spiral stairway was there room for the three of us to gather around a little table for breakfast. Close quarters probably didn't faze the usual chalet clientele—speleologists.

Fittingly, as we came down into the valley of the Bouigane there was a great kennel of spotted hunting dogs. This was the country of Gaston Phoebus, a rather nasty fourteenth-century count. He had his brother assassinated, killed his son during an argument, and at the age of sixty was still in hand-to-hand combat with bears. He also specialized in hunting with dogs, wrote a treatise on the subject, and raised six hundred hunting dogs. Perhaps these were descendants of Gaston's canines.

At Orgibet, there'd been a wedding the day before. We stopped for a cafe snack, and the happy mother of the groom outdid herself for us. Eve and I asked for soup. It came in an enormous tureen. Jim asked for a sandwich. It came in the form of a basket of bread and two large platters of ham and cold meats. It was all left over from the wedding feast. Nothing would do but that we have some of the wedding cake too—and, for Eve a Jordan almond, good luck sign at French nuptials.

Madame told us that during the World War II bombing of Le Havre she had lost every member of her family. Her face was drawn and sad. But a moment later she gave a little jump and philosophized: "Mais on est bien, il y a de l'air, on est ici." ("But one is all right, there is air, one is here.") How could that be improved upon?

Castillon was a mail stop, but the post office had closed for the day. The next day would be Eve's eighteenth birthday, and our plan, worked out at Luchon, called for an overnight side trip.

After breakfast, as arranged, a car and driver came for us. We were to spend two days like ordinary people, traveling to Foix by way of the great cave of Mas d'Azil, and back to Castillon by way of Labouiche. From Foix we'd visit the Niaux caves.

I hurried over to the post office to pick up the mail before we left, and as I sat in the back seat of the car, reading first of all David's letter from Alaska, my stomach turned several flip-flops.

Having two days off duty from his Forest Service work on the Kenai Peninsula, he'd gone on an overnight fishing trip alone. Hiking back the second morning, he rounded a bend in the trail and saw a giant Kodiak bear and her cub.

> As soon as I saw her, I froze. She turned and saw me and immediately charged. I allowed her to get about ten feet from me, then shot at her head with my .357 magnum (revolver). After I shot, she swerved and ran on past, turned, and charged again. I again fired at the head at about ten feet, causing her to swerve past me again. She charged a third time. I fired, and she swerved past me. She hesitated before charging again, and during that time I immediately shed my packboard and camera. She charged a fourth time, and I again fired at the head, and she swerved to the side and ran on by. She did not charge again, and I immediately climbed a tree. From the tree, I looked in all directions, and saw nothing more of the bear or the cub. After waiting in the tree about twenty minutes, I came down, reloaded my gun from my pack, and continued down the trail. As I passed the spot where I had first seen the bear and cub, I saw what were apparently the remains of a moose.

Climbing down the tree, he wondered how he had gotten up it so fast. "And I'm mighty grateful," he wrote, "for all those sessions of pistol practice in the basement!"

A CAVEY BIRTHDAY

AT Foix, we arranged, or thought we arranged, to meet Monsieur Casteret at two, on the square at Tarascon, to be guided by him through the caves at Niaux.

"He's very famous," I informed Jim and Eve. "He discovered half the caves in the Pyrenees. He's the one who put the coloring matter in the water way up there to prove where the Garonne comes from. We're really in luck to have such a distinguished man all to ourselves as guide."

It turned out that "Monsieur Casteret" was Monsieur Clastre and that we and thirty-seven other people were to have him "all to ourselves." We gulped and instructed our driver to follow the cavalcade.

At the cave entrance we were marshalled and sorted out with *une lampe chaque deux personnes* ("one carbide lamp for every two people"). Naturally by the time they got to us the lamps were all gone. But Jim, with his usual forethought, had brought a flashlight, so we wriggled in after the others. The opening was just a shade larger than the one marked with James Brace's obituary.

Stalactites, stalagmites. Drawings of horses, bisons, reindeer, mountain sheep, and even "road maps"—diagrams of the caves—all drawn with a mixture of bison grease and oxide of manganese! It was two hours in another world, the world of the Magdalenian period.

Before starting back toward the entrance, M. Clastre joked, in the rehearsed way of guides, that if *messieurs et mesdames* wanted to crawl through holes on their stomachs, wade through icy water up to their hips, and *grimper* on hands and knees up slick-as-oil slopes, he could take us on through and get us out at the mouth of a different, connecting cave, the Grotte de Lombrives—before midnight. Plan rejected with groans and giggles.

With birthday champagne for dinner, we waxed philosophical. While we didn't regret not having crawled through to Lombrives, we couldn't put out of our minds the Albigensians who'd made the cave their cathedral, and been walled up inside it by the thirteenth-century "new crusaders" to starve there, along with their bishop. That was their choice, rather than submit to the Pope.

We weighed the pros and cons of taking one's convictions that seriously. Was an abstract religious tenet worth giving up the priceless gift of life? And why couldn't people in the thirteenth century, or for that matter the twentieth, live and let live?

Labouiche had for us next day more caves, but with a difference. Here was the longest navigable underground river in the world. At 226 feet beneath the surface, we traveled more than two miles in metal boats, through caves—some wide, some narrow, some high vaulted, and some low ceilinged.

It was all well illuminated, except in two instances: the first, when the guide-boatman switched off the lights to convey what it had been like for the discoverers and explorers of Labouiche; the second, when the lights simply went out. "Ne bougez pas, messieurs 'dames!" he said quickly, in a tone of great urgency. "Ne bougez pas!" ("Don't budge.") Budging was farthest from our thoughts.

The lights came on again. One of the other guides, he explained, must have thrown the wrong switch and then rectified it. Perhaps. Or perhaps just good theater. In any case, it was worth the price of admission.

DIVIDE CONQUERED

AFTER two days of investigating caves and subterranean rivers, we were in love with earth's surface, sky, clouds, and sun. And after 160 miles of automobile travel, we were still in love with walking.

Our trail, picked up again at Castillon and following down the Lez River valley, with lush abundant farms and rows of Lombardy poplars, was an idyll. The notion of stopping in at the National Center of Scientific Research in the Grotte de Moulis, to see how they study cave-dwelling animals, filled us with an overpowering indifference.

Beyond St-Girons, our road, an old back road, followed the Salat River upstream, taking us out of the old province of Comminges and into the Comté de Foix. The broad fertile valley was soon squeezed into a narrow gorge with steep thicketed slopes. Perched on rocks and wading in the rapids with rod and net were *amateurs de la pêche,* whose wives could usually be seen sitting in the car or on the bank, knitting.

Every twist and turn of the river, which was now the Arac, was matched by a twist or turn of the road. It was thirsty work and we anticipated a cafe stop at Kercabanac, which had made its appearance on the official milestones. But there was no cafe at Kercabanac because, oh woe, Kercabanac was a tunnel. Seated at the mouth of Kercabanac we refreshed ourselves from canteen and knapsack.

At Biert a *pétanque* game was in progress in the wide place in the street that served as square. It was the first *pétanque* game in which we'd seen a woman play. In principle, it was good. But she needed more practice, a lot more.

Pétanque, or *boules,* is the national everyman's warm-weather sport of France. People own their own sets of balls, take them along on vacation. There are village tournaments in the *place,* or next to the church, or beside the cafe, or wherever a reasonably flat piece of ground is available.

Pétanque is like horseshoes played with balls. The rules are many and complex, the fine points very fine. You can "point" your ball—that is, try to roll it so it will come to a halt as close as possible to the little ball. Or "fire" the ball so as to knock your opponent's ball away from the little one. Or "fire" at the little one, *le but* ("the target"), so as to knock it away from the opponent's ball and closer to one of yours.

Played singles or by teams of up to four, a hotly contested game of *boules* will draw dozens of spectators, and often a good deal of time is spent in discussing the best way to approach the next throw, analyzing the last throw, projecting what the outcome would have been "if—." And so on. The two teams may go into the cafe after the game and, over drinks paid for by the losers, rehash everything and decide then to go out and play another match—though darkness may be falling.

Set into the front of a house across from the *boules* court was what appeared to be a stone mask. What did it signify? No one could tell us. A bit farther, beside the road, was an ancient stone head in a kind of stone niche, and on it the date 1290. About that, too, we drew a blank.

Had there been some medieval chateau near here, some fortress-castle that was razed and pillaged? How had the stone mask and the stone head gotten where they were? The head, with its niche, must have weighed a good four hundred pounds. How could people live right on top of puzzles like these and rest without solving them?

Hail to Europe's most tireless travelers, the Belgians and the Dutch! We were always bumping into parties of them. It was hardly surprising that the town of Massat had guests from Antwerp, Brussels, and Liège, for the hotel was run by Belgians. *Monsieur le chef* held numerous citations for his *haute cuisine*—surest way of keeping a hotel filled.

A Belgian couple invited us to join them for after-dinner cognacs. "It will make you sleep well," said the woman to me. Little did she know what I could do, without cognac, in the way of sleeping, after twenty-seven-and-a-half kilometers.

I was recounting to her in French how we managed clothing matters on a walking trip. Meaning to say that every night I washed the socks *(chaussettes)*, I said with perfect poise, "Chaque soir je lave les chaussées." ("Every night I wash the pavements.")

Another Sunday had come around. While church bells rang at Massat, outside our window a shepherd with a Long John Silver peg leg sat on a folding chair while his dog worked the cows and sheep. Busy whittling something, the old man occasionally looked up to whistle or shout his instructions, which were promptly obeyed.

It was bright, with brilliant white clouds and a breeze. Ahead of us lay a two-*col* day. The first, Caougnous, was scarcely noticeable, so low and gentle was it.

Although Col de Port was only 4,060 feet above the sea, lower than several *cols* we'd already crossed, it marked the Atlantic-Mediterranean watershed.

The gradient was a trifling 5 percent. As always, simply putting one foot in front of the other did the job. Forest gave way to grass and ferns, and tile roofs to thatch. Presently we were at the summit, with its windswept moors and knobs, with its ferns and heather, with its Sunday-outing people wandering here and there. Behind us, the predominantly green and gently modeled mountains of the Atlantic watershed. Before us, the more severe, the rockier, more barren Mediterranean watershed.

A large family gathering at the Café du Col gave the place a festive air. Talk, laughter, jukebox music, and the clatter of dishes filled the place. We shared a table with that *rara avis* in France, a Protestant minister, and his wife.

Our soup grew cold while we gave autographs to some young people who'd seen our picture in *La Dépêche*.

From the minister's wife I sought the meaning of a roadside sign that had been puzzling me: *Asticot Interdit*. As familiar to us as *Défense d'Uriner* were *Entrée Interdite* ("no admittance"), *Publicité Interdite* ("post no bills"), and *Cracher Interdit* ("spitting prohibited"). But what was *Asticot Interdit*? Jim's pocket dictionary had been no help. If only we knew what *asticot* meant, we had sometimes thought, we might like to try it and see if it was really a fun thing.

"Ah, asticot!" said the minister's wife. "Oui! Asticot interdit!" It meant you couldn't use maggots for bait.

Fortified with new knowledge, with tepid soup, and with the self-esteem of amateur autograph givers, we sallied forth into the Mediterranean landscape.

Hardly was the cafe out of sight when a small girl came panting after us. Her *maman* had sent her to give us each an *écusson*. *Maman* had no doubt observed that, sewn to our knapsacks, were a colorful array of small felt coats of arms from many of the places on our walking trips. She wanted us to include Col de Port, with its isard silhouetted against mountains and sky.

It was down, down, down, then, through a sunny valley to Saurat, where church bells were ringing so insistently that, thinking there must be some special mass, we went in. There was no mass, just one old woman in black, praying. I sat there in the cool darkness, reflecting on how strongly a place of worship can influence worship itself.

It was market day the next day at Luzenac, on up the Ariège valley. There was the poultry girl with her live chickens and ducks, resting herself on an upturned bucket while her charges clucked and quacked in the shade. There was one of her satisfied customers, carrying her dissatisfied purchase by its feet. There was the man weighing mushrooms in a big scale and then wrapping them in the leaves of an old *Paris-Match*. There were the three old men who'd clubbed together to buy a cask of wine and, now that it was loaded onto the wheelbarrow, were trying to decide who should push it. There was the fish market, with fishes so big they must have come from the Mediterranean.

How would you cook that fish, I asked the man. (Not that I planned to buy it.) In oil, naturally, he told me, in olive oil. Had I not heard the saying, "Il faut que le poisson meure dans l'huile comme il est né dans l'eau" ("The fish must die in oil as it is born in water")?

"Sure proof we're near the Mediterranean," said Jim. "From now on we'll be lubricated to death with oil of olives."

Andorra was a bit more than fifty miles off to the side from Ax-les-Thermes. Andorra—the mini-principality with feudal customs still surviving, with its coprotectors the Bishop of Urgel and the President of France, with its militia of sixteen men! To arrive there on foot had been a dream of long standing. But to get up and over the pass would be a steep, shadeless, waterless business—a hard two-day hike with only one outpost of civilization en route. We just didn't have what it would take.

Worse luck, Andorra was one of our mail stops. Now this singular mini-state has a double postal system, and common sense told us if we wanted our mail we'd have to go for it in person.

A hired car and driver the next day took us over and back. There was no mail anyway, at either the French or the Spanish post office, and (though the country was magnificent) the city, Andorra-la-Vella, was a tourist trap par excellence. Jammed with people who'd come to take advantage of the favorable exchange, it was made up almost exclusively of hotels, restaurants, bars, and souvenir shops. Crack went a dream. All we could say in Andorra's favor was that for once we'd gotten our fill of olives.

APRÈS LE DÉLUGE

BACK in Ax-les-Thermes, we didn't linger. We'd seen other spas along the way.

The Col de Chioula was our introduction to Sault, a high plateau region celebrated for its forests, its mean winds, and the general rudesse of its climate. A thermometer on the *col* registered 100 degrees, rude enough.

Down off the *col* and in the valley of the Hers nestled the hamlet of Prades. Unfortunately, it was not the Prades of Pablo Casals, but a smaller and quite insignificant Prades. We wanted very much to get out of the rude Sault sun and cool off, but there was no sign of a cafe.

An old man asked what we were searching for and immediately took us under his wing. "Suivez-moi." We followed him through a back alley, into a dark stable where we barely made out three forms standing in stalls. A moo told us they were cows. Our old guide, who'd evidently been here hundreds of times, faltered not. We groped our way after him up a stairway which issued into a family kitchen containing, in addition to the dinner table in the center, two small tables. We took one, he the other. Two daughters of the family served us some pop and, without asking, brought him *un pinard,* a glass of ordinary red wine. These people were obviously operating without a license, but, with the pungent odor of cow manure that came up between the floorboards, it seemed unlikely they could ever do a roaring business or cheat the government out of many francs.

As we drank our lemon and orange drinks, our friend joined one of the girls to look out the window. There was a storm coming, they said.

We paid, put on our knapsacks, thanked him, and felt our way down into the stable. The cows—did I imagine it?—seemed restless.

Ominous dark clouds were scudding toward us from the southwest. "If we put on some speed," I suggested, "maybe we can get out of its path."

"It won't last long anyway," said Jim. "It'll be one of those brief half-hearted drizzles."

"Hope you're right," Eve commented. "Those people we just passed were saying we're going to have *une douche formidable.*"

Racing that storm was like racing a locomotive. When it overtook us, shortly after we got out of Prades, it struck like a ton of bricks, and it lasted more than a half hour. The blast jackets, hastily pulled from the knapsacks, were soaked through in short order. Their tight elastic wristbands collected water up inside the sleeves, so that our arms resembled fat red, blue, and green sausages. Not a tree in sight, even though this was Sault, land of forests! Not a shed, not a ruin, not a shelter of any kind, and by now too far to go back to Prades. And too humiliating.

We tried standing close together under a slightly overhanging clay bank. The rain found us there just the same, and all we got was some rare abstract designs, in clay, on our backs.

Should we try to get out the raincoats? It would just get everything in the knapsacks wet. The coats might be doing some good in there, and we were already soaked. Best to keep moving, we decided, stay warm, and get on toward our goal for the night. On we slogged, with the deluge letting up not one drop.

At last a village hove into view: Camurac, complete with hotel. Water pouring from us, we walked into the bar and asked if they could serve us some hot coffee. "Rien de plus facile," replied the bartender. ("Nothing easier.")

We stood there while the young man at his extreme leisure washed, wiped, and polished glasses, gossiping and joking with his customers. Finally he started three *caffè espressos* on their interminable trickle, drop by sluggish drop, into three small cups. When at last they stood before us on the bar, about two-thirds full and lukewarm, our teeth were chattering and our hands were so numb we could scarcely lift the cups.

Perhaps it was the caffein, or the being in a warm room for a few minutes, or just possibly the cognac that as an afterthought we'd had him add. Whatever it was, we left Camurac not quite so dispirited. Still drenched to the skin and bedraggled, however, we didn't take it kindly that some people drew their car up alongside us as we walked, and without a by-your-leave, took movies of us. The guidebook had said the climate thereabouts was rude. It hadn't mentioned the people.

Our two rooms at Belcaire were soon a weird sight. Within minutes, up went my rubber clothesline and onto it its capacity in wet clothes. Other wet things were draped over every object that dampness would not damage, for almost everything in our knapsacks had gotten soaked. Things that had taken on the least moisture were hung nearest the light bulbs in the hope they'd be dry enough to wear to dinner. Jim requested an extra towel for his beard. My camera and attachments were all laid open to air. With Madame's permission I put my watch, from which I'd removed the back, into the oven for a few brief moments.

All in all, it had been an absorbing experience.

TO EAT IS TO MAKE HISTORY

TWICE the next day we saw rainbows. Though we went up and down two *cols*, they were lower, the country was flatter. We were really working toward the lip of the cup that was the Mediterranean. Through woods and through farmland, we ticked off the kilometers. Through showers, through sunshine, through wind.

Again people stopped their cars beside us. They'd seen us on television. One party offered us a ride; another wanted to carry our knapsacks on ahead. After some 440 miles of integrity, we should spoil our record now!

Cypresses, those most south-of-France trees, heralded the approach

of Quillan. It looked good to us after thirty-three kilometers—so good
that we decided on a day's layover there.

One of the great hat-making centers of France, Quillan owes its
preeminence in that field to inhabitants of nearby Bugarach, who in
1804 returned home from Upper Silesia, where they'd been prisoners
of war and where they'd learned the art of making fine felt *chapeaux*.
The trend toward going bareheaded was hurting Quillan's hat industry, but there were other arts there.

It was in Quillan that we met Señor D. Ibañez, Spanish sculptor
and woodworker. Wandering through forest and along seashore, he
gathered pieces of deadwood and driftwood that were *suggestifs* of
animals, brought them back in his truck, amended them with his
chisel, polished and titled them.

Still another Quillan art was surely the culinary art, for on the
wall of the hotel dining room was lettered in all seriousness: La cuisine française est la meilleure du monde. Cette gloire éclatera par-
dessus les autres quand l'humanité, plus sage, mettra la broche au
dessus de l'épée." ("French cooking is the best in the world. This
glory will shine forth above all others when humanity, become wiser,
puts the spit above the sword.")

We couldn't quarrel with the ultimate aim of a world without
war. Nor could we deny that French cooking is tasty. Nor could we
even find fault with the implied self-glorification. We had five delicious meals in that room under that elegantly lettered motto.

The more I learned about French cuisine, however, the more
convinced I became that I didn't have the makings of a gourmet cook.
The cooking pot that must never be washed and never allowed to
grow cold? I'd be unable to resist giving it a good scrub once in a
while; I'd forget and let it get cold. The verse one was supposed to
say while mixing salad dressings, the first line for the oil and the second for the vinegar? I'd get it backwards. My French blood surely
was not the blood of great chefs.

A sign on a tree caught our attention: *Mariages—à l'Embarras,*
du Choix—Rousset—à St-Julia-de-Bec. ("Marriages, an embarrassment
of choices!") There was apparently a marriage broker named Rousset
in St-Julia-de-Bec, some three kilometers distant. We were tempted to
turn aside for St-Julia just to see what sort of establishment it might
be, what sort of person Monsieur or Madame Rousset might be. But
it was to be a nearly thirty-five-kilometer day—more than twenty-one
miles. It seemed like a poor time to add mileage, since none of us
was seriously interested in finding a spouse just then.

At Ax-les-Thermes we'd left the really high Pyrenees, and we were
now walking in the foothills and their gentle valleys. It was raincoat
weather. Between showers we sat on a wall for bread and sausage.

Soon, after a magnificent pine forest, we found ourselves climbing Col St-Louis. Off to the side and snugly cupped in a green depression was St-Louis village: whitewashed houses with tile roofs, a dream village.

Wild wind blowing tall grass met us at the summit, and below was a landscape of bright gray and rose gray rock, cypresses, and scrub pine, and, arching over all, the bluest of skies with the whitest of clouds.

The descent, down the steep narrow rocky Défilé de Pierre Lys, brought into view a great viaduct of modern construction but with Roman lines. In one of those fascinating tours de force that make engineering seem magic to laymen, the road went across the viaduct, doubled back on itself, and then went under the viaduct.

Beyond the ruins of a Moorish castle, we were skirting a cliff when Eve noticed a plaque set in the rock. *Ici M. le Duc et Mme la Duchesse d'Orléans Ont Déjeuné le 5–7–1839.* Who but the French would think of erecting a monument to a picnic? Ah, long live the spit supreme!

TO ALL GOOD THINGS . . .

NOW we were walking in an endless expanse of vineyards, miles upon miles of them, with their broad, beautifully shaped leaves, with their clusters of juice-heavy grapes coming to purple ripeness under the Mediterranean sun. Having left mountain magnificence behind us, we couldn't have devised a more idyllic setting for the final days of our promenade.

Through the open gate of one vineyard we glimpsed a deserted chateau and half expected to see at one of its tall, glassless windows some aristocratic ghost.

Caudies, as we approached it, looked like a medieval village, hugging the edge of a cliff above the Maury River. Some of its dark stone houses had only a single tiny window cut into the massive back wall.

And now a cruel fate. After hours on the quiet back road through vineyards, we had to join the highway, which was not a wide one. Traffic was heavy for it was Sunday. Back to the old formula of shouting "Over!" whenever cars were about to pass too close.

A couple of hours later, the almost inevitable confronted us. Traffic was backed up at least a kilometer behind a four-car crash, and two ambulances, sounding their blood-curdling sirens, streaked past us to where the curious had crowded around the wreckage and the injured.

This was one sight we could forgo, and we bypassed it by walking through a vineyard—sorry for the circumstances, glad for the excuse.

At St-Paul-de-Fenouillet, where the church had a very Byzantine look, dinner was served in a glassed-in porch with a bamboo ceiling and a fine fig tree looking in. Toward coffee time, one of three gentlemen at a nearby table stepped over and offered us cigarettes, in English. Surprised, Jim thanked him and, wishing to please, added, "You speak English very well."

"I'm an Englishman," he replied.

A good laugh, and we spent the next hour or so with them. One was a science teacher, one a headmaster, and one a retired chap. What he'd retired from, neither of the others seemed to know, and, considering that they were all traveling together, it struck us this was carrying British reticence a bit far, what?

The next three days were to be in the nature of a final dash to the sea, highway all the way. We'd have minded more, had it not been such a beautiful, fruitful land.

It was vineyards all the way to Estagel and hot and windy. Here and there, berry bushes growing in hedges made pleasant dallying points. Mindful of the snake Eve had seen on a wall (posterior six inches only, and disappearing rapidly) we were careful where we put hands and feet.

Il Est Défendu, said a sign on the outskirts of Maury, *sous Peine d'Amende de Trotter dans l'Intérieur de la Ville.* ("It is forbidden on pain of fine to trot in the interior of the city.") Exercising great self-control, we did not trot.

At a huge cooperative winery in Maury, we invited ourselves in and were kindly received by the supervisor, who showed us all the great casks, the vats, testing equipment, and so on. He tried to present us with a bottle of Maury, but we weren't in the mood to add that much weight to our load. Instead, sitting us down in the delightful cool of the vast stone building, he served us each a glass of this delicious red wine.

This was the heart of Roussillon, one of France's coming wine regions. For generations wine grapes have been grown and wine has been made there, but only rather recently have Roussillon vintages been the object of demand from outside. "The secret of their difference," the supervisor told us, "is that, because of the favorable exposure and climate, these grapes always attain full maturity, with a very high content of grape sugar." The Maury we sampled was like a fortified Burgundy, but no brandy had been added: its 16 percent alcoholic content was the result of natural fermentation.

As the afternoon wore on the wind got wilder. It was the tramontane, second only to the world famous mistral. Had there been no railing on the bridge over the Maury, three Americans might have landed in the river with all their belongings.

But Estagel, with its tile roofs, its bougainvilleas, its cypresses, its fig and olive trees, seemed quite oblivious to the tramontane. People in shorts went about their business, placidly righting things that blew over, greeting each other casually, as though this near-tornadic wind were a mere spring zephyr. We made for the hotel.

Oui, said the maid, they had reserved rooms for us, but only *Madame la patronne* knew which ones and she was reposing herself. Could we come back in three-quarters of an hour?

My blood, already hot, neared the boiling point.

Jim—calmer, wiser, and always more of a diplomat—offhandedly remarked that *Madame la patronne* had doubtless seen us on television but didn't realize it was we who'd made the reservation.

Presto! The maid disappeared, reappeared, and showed us to our rooms. Such is fame.

After the wind died down there was time for a walk around Estagel. Scaffolding stood around the twelfth-century church which was being rebuilt. That any structure could have survived the tramontane for eight centuries was beyond belief. Here and there in Estagel small statues of the Virgin stood in niches in walls. Rows of cane served as fences and windbreaks. The setting sun gilded a hillside above the town, where the annual *cargolade* ("snail bake") is held. Mauve colored lees (dregs) of wine lay spread in drying grounds, eventually to be transformed into cream of tartar and an infection-fighting drug.

Barcelona was coming loud and clear over someone's radio in the street even before we were up the next day, adding to the holiday spirit that filled us, because Perpignan, big city of the eastern Pyrenees, was our goal for the day. After that, the Mediterranean was but a stone's throw.

A man we met coming from his vineyard stopped to chat and insisted on giving us several bunches of grapes. Elsewhere, a fig tree spread its branches temptingly over me.

"May I?"

"If it's over the road," Jim replied, "it's legally yours, or anybody's." I hoped that on this point French law was the same as American. In two seconds I had picked a fig, whipped out my pocket knife, and peeled it. It was fat, it was sweet, moist, creamy.

"Bon courage," someone called to us.

At eleven o'clock we surmounted our last, our twentieth *col,* La

Dona. It was only two hundred meters above the sea, but high enough so that at 11:10 Eve cried out, "I see Perpignan! That must be the Perpignan water tower!" It was true.

Vineyards continued, with their small shelters built of cypress and cane, or rock and cane, in which a vineyard worker could take refuge from sun or rain. Off to one side, up a rocky road, stood an old monastery, or winery, or monastery-winery.

The terrain flattened and, mixed in with vineyards now, were orchards and truck gardens.

At Pezilla de la Rivière where we stopped for refreshment, the cafe host presented Eve and me with a beautiful melon and Jim with a glass of wine. This was southern hospitality. (And male chauvinism?) Throughout Pezilla's extensive trailer camp for migrant pickers were tall stacks of four-handled baskets for the tomatoes, the melons, the peaches.

It was hot, hot, hot. It had to be, to ripen and perfect all this natural bounty!

At St-Estève, a single giant sycamore spread its shade over almost the whole village square, and a small iron table stood under it.

"Meant for us." And we piled our knapsacks at the foot of the tree. Nothing but ice cream would do. Eve went into the cafe to order *glaces,* and I went to a small bakery up the street for *tortillons,* a regional cookie.

The bakery lady had evidently observed our arrival and our bivouacking under the sycamore. "Il est plus facile de sortir par ici," she told me (it would be easier to go out the other door). She led me through a room, white with flour, where innumerable loaves were rising on rows and rows of shelves. "Merci, Madame," she thanked me. "Bon appétit." If anyone ever wasted words it was those gracious people who wished us good appetite.

The closer we got to Perpignan, a city of seventy thousand, the thicker the traffic. Added to the usual big city traffic were truckloads of tomatoes and truckloads of peaches going to the cannery and trucks loaded with empty baskets going back to orchard and field.

Despite Perpignan's noise we slept well, content in our hearts. We knew that with another 13 kilometers the next day we were going to have completed 504 miles, our longest walking trip.

It was a half-day romp down to the shore at Canet-Plage, and at the town limits of the beach resort, Eve and I ritualistically threw away our hats.

"For shame!" cried Jim. "When I threw my tweed hat from the Jacques Cartier Bridge at Montreal, you all howled."

"This is different," we chimed.

"My hat cost $2.89," I said. "Look at it. It doesn't owe me a thing."

"Mine cost four dollars," said Eve, "and after what it's been through I wouldn't ask a dog to wear it."

"Ladies, you have the last word."

The sand was pale gold. Beyond and above it spread the bluest blues of sea and sky. Off to the southwest, Mont Canigou, nine thousand feet high and the last high peak at this end of the Pyrenees, reared its crest above the surrounding landscape. Due south, Roc de France, lower but still imposing, dipped its very toes in the sea.

Hands joined, the three of us walked across the beach to the Mediterranean. The kids had grown up. We could not expect, ever again, another family walking trip. Nothing like it would ever happen again.

But what we'd had, nothing in the world could ever take away from us.